Life
Interrupted

Donna M. McCully

Donna M. McCully

No part of this book may be reproduced, stored in a retrieval system, or transmitted in any form or by any means, electronic, mechanical, photocopying, recording, or otherwise, without the prior written permission of the publisher. Unauthorized use or distribution of this book is strictly prohibited and may result in legal action.

Donna M. McCully. All right reserved @2024

Dedication

I dedicate this book to my wonderful husband. Sedrick, I think about you daily and wish you were still here to share my life. You are gone too soon, and I will always love you. Your cherished memories will live on in my heart. Thank you for being the most caring, loving husband a woman could ask for. My darling, may you rest in peace.

Also, I dedicate this book to my beloved parents. God blessed me with a wonderful mother and father who helped shape me into the woman I am today. Thank you both for your love and guidance and your thoughtfulness. You will always be in my heart. I miss you dearly! Even though God took you home, I hope to see you and Sedrick again someday.

Megan and Mary-Jane, my dearest cousins, I love you both with all my heart, and I am so happy that we stay in touch.

To Georgia, Alan, and Kati, thank you for welcoming my father into your family with open arms and showing him so much love in his golden years.

To Cari, Sylvain, Mona, Jaffer, Sharon, Roger, Jill, Heidi, Gail, Roberte, and Roma, your treasured friendship means the world to me, more than you will ever know. You are always there for me. Thank you all for your love, kindness, support, and encouragement through the darkest times of my life. I am so grateful for all of you.

Lily, thank you so much for taking such great care of my dad all the years you worked for him. He greatly valued your friendship as well. You and I share a special bond.

To Jean, thank you so much for being my dad's good friend and pool buddy. He used to enjoy swimming up and down in the pool with you, telling you stories about what his

Donna M. McCully

life was like in his younger years and all the changes he had seen during his lifetime. He always looked forward to those early morning swims and lively conversations with you, rain or shine.

In loving memory of my dear cat Mojo, a great source of comfort and joy for almost ten years. He will always be special to me.

For my newly adopted cat, Breezie, who puts a smile on my face daily. I love her so much.

To all who read this book, thank you for giving my words a chance and letting me share my truth.

Life Interrupted

Contents

Dedication iii

Introduction 1

Chapter 1 Evil Bursts Through the Door 3

Chapter 2 My Beautiful Husband Shot 15

Chapter 3 Our Home, Now A Major Crime Scene 21

Chapter 4 The Aftermath 29

Chapter 5 Planning A Painful Farewell 43

Chapter 6 Our Love Story 46

Chapter 7 Ominous Warning Signs 52

Chapter 8 Laying My Husband to Rest 57

Chapter 9 First Christmas Without My Beloved 63

Chapter 10 Facing Sudden Widowhood 67

Chapter 11 Dad's Grim Diagnosis 71

Chapter 12 Rapid Decline 73

Chapter 13 Dad Loses His Battle with Dementia 80

Chapter 14 Preparing for A Second Sad Farewell 89

Chapter 15 Dad's Story 92

Chapter 16 The Celebration of Life Ceremony 98

Chapter 17 In Survivor Mode 102

Chapter 18 Finding Comfort in Faith 109

Chapter 19 First Anniversary of Sedrick's Death 111

Chapter 20 Leaving Jamaica Behind 113

Chapter 21 Turning the Page 117

Chapter 22 The Relentless Grip of Grief and Trauma............. 122

Chapter 23 The Murder Investigation 127

Chapter 24 Lessons Learned About Moving Abroad 133

Chapter 25 Putting Down New Roots 136

Chapter 26 Surviving Breast Cancer 139

Chapter 27 10 Years After Sedrick's Murder 143

Introduction

When you lose someone you love, it stays with you.

My name is Donna Marie McCully, and I am a homicide survivor. This book is a true story of my lived experience. Some names were changed to protect privacy.

I wrote this book partly because I thought it would be therapeutic. For anyone who has ever experienced the violent death of a loved one, grief is overwhelmingly unbearable and complicated. When someone you love dies, it is one of the worst trials you can suffer in life, and for anyone who feels hopeless in their grief, I share in your pain and sorrow.

It has been painful for me to write about the tragic events that have shattered my life, but it comes right from the very depths of my heart and soul. My memoir is about the senseless murder of my beloved husband, Sedrick. It is also about what it was like to lose my Dad, Eloi McCully. He was present during the murder, and it greatly affected him. I lost him to the cruel grip of dementia in the months following Sedrick's murder.

My heart is still heavy with the weight of unspeakable loss. Each word on these pages is a testament to the pain of losing those dearest to me, yet amidst the darkness, a flicker of resilience emerges. Grief has many manifestations, and each one of them has a different effect on our soul, affecting us in weird ways. Giving these weird feelings words is hard, but it might just be easier to relate to them, for in pain, we are equal; we all hurt the same. Through my story, I offer solace to those who tread the lonely path of grief, a reminder that even in the face of unimaginable sorrow, the human spirit endures.

These events have changed my life forever and made me

look at life differently. Life following the death of your dear ones can and does go on, even though it is a very long, arduous journey. I will now share my story with you and how I have coped.

donnamarie.mccully@gmail.com

Life Interrupted

Chapter 1
Evil Bursts Through the Door

It all changes in a blink; all the happiness drowns in sorrow, leaving us tainted on the inside, a broken shell devoid of life and emotions.

Sunday, November 17, 2013, was a day that brought me unbelievable pain and heartache and was etched into my brain forever. As is typical in Jamaica, the morning was sunny and tranquil, and you could hear nightingales singing cheerful songs. We lived in the lovely neighborhood of Huddersfield, which is in the Parish of St. Mary on the North Coast of Jamaica. My husband Sedrick and I moved to our dream home beside the sparkling turquoise waters of the Caribbean Sea in August 2012. We bought an empty lot there in 2003, and it had taken almost ten years to finish building the house.

Sedrick, who was born in Jamaica, immigrated to Canada in 1980. Due to economic and political problems in Jamaica during that time, he wanted to go to Canada to try and make a better life for himself. After living in Toronto temporarily with some of his cousins, he settled in Ottawa with his sister Sheila. When he first moved to Ottawa, he worked for a moving company before taking a job as a maintenance worker at the University of Ottawa.

After we got married, he took a course in electronics and had been employed in the high-tech industry as a certified electronics assembler for several years. However, high-tech slowed down, and eventually, he got laid off. Sedrick was always a very hard worker and got hired as a contract worker in different high-tech firms. In between, he also took some laborer jobs in construction and a truck driver position delivering food to the University of Ottawa.

I worked as a clerk in various departments within the Federal Public Service. Due to budget constraints, the Federal Government cut several positions in 2012. At the time, I was working for the Canada Border Services Agency as a Human Resources Assistant, and my department had also been affected by the layoffs. I got offered an early retirement package. I was 50 years old, and Sedrick and I decided to move to Jamaica while we were both still young and healthy enough to enjoy it. We had each worked a total of thirty-two years and were both tired of the long, cold Ottawa winters. We had dreamed of starting a new life together in Jamaica, and this seemed like the perfect time.

I was so excited at the prospect of not having to see any more winters but waking up to look at the beautiful sea every day. On the last day of work, my manager Mona and my co-workers threw a lovely retirement party for me, and their thoughtfulness touched me. Everyone was so thrilled for me to have the opportunity to move to Jamaica.

On August 16, 2012, we landed in Montego Bay and drove to our new home. We chose to live in this neighborhood because it is a quiet, upscale neighborhood of mostly returning residents. The tourist town of Ocho Rios is just a 10-minute drive away and has many popular attractions, including Dunns River Falls, Dolphin Cove, and Mystic Mountain, to name a few.

It is almost funny when I think back on all the joy I felt at our new home, the laughter, the many moments of serenity; I had taken everything for granted; it never occurred to me then, not even once that soon it all would go up in smoke, my precious happy home, I would become homeless within it. Marriage is a sacred pact; home begins and ends with our spouse; imagining a life without them may sound offensive and corny, but it hurts more than anything and everything combined. The hardest part is continuing, knowing that it will never be the same.

Sedrick decided that he would like to drive a tourist bus in Jamaica and to be able to work for himself for a change. We both thought he could make a decent income, especially with all the nearby tourist attractions. After living in Jamaica for a few months, we purchased a 15-seat Toyota minibus. He joined the JUTA Tours bus company and had begun driving tourists to and from the Kingston and Montego Bay airports to a few different resorts. Sedrick was an outgoing, friendly, charming man who seemed to fit into the tourist business. He wanted to drive the bus for just a few years, and then we would sell it or split the weekly earnings with another driver who would operate the bus instead of Sedrick. We planned to spend some time travelling to a few different countries that we had always wanted to go and see. He even talked about starting a small recycling business in Jamaica because there was so little recycling on the island. Sedrick loved the environment and wanted to be able to do something that could make a difference to help reduce pollution on the island.

I remember the first trip that he took as a JUTA driver. The Manager of JUTA for the Ocho Rios branch called Sedrick one morning in early October to send him to pick up a few tourists from one of the all-inclusive resorts. He was to bring them to Sangster's International Airport in Montego Bay. Sedrick was a bit nervous and asked me to accompany him. I thought it would be fun to go along, and I joined him. He was tall and slim and looked sharp in his black pants and crisp white shirt that morning. The trip went very smoothly without any problems. He talked with the tourists on the bus, asking them where they were from and if they had enjoyed themselves in Jamaica. They were all in a great mood and happy to chat with him. As we turned onto the road leading to the airport, he smiled and told everyone that it was his first trip. Then he thanked them all for giving him their business. They all clapped, said he had done a great job, and thanked him for getting them to the airport safely and in plenty of time to catch their flights. He had picked up a few more tourists to bring back to the hotel on the return trip. I felt so proud of him and knew he had found his niche. We were planning on eventually developing a website so he could book trips directly with tourists from overseas. After that first trip, he had only been driving the bus for six weeks, and our future looked promising. The manager of JUTA Tours gave him a lot of work because he said Sedrick was very courteous and liked his attitude. Sadly, the poor man would never even be able to collect his first paycheck.

    I had watched Sedrick come alive in his element. Yet beneath the veneer of poise, I sensed the subtle tremor of nerves, the silent prayer for everything to go smoothly. As he engaged with the tourists, my heart swelled with pride. His voice rang out with a mix of genuine curiosity and hospitality, eager to connect with them beyond the norm. Each conversation was a bridge built between strangers to charm and disarm with his warmth.

Life Interrupted

    We had picked up my father, Eloi, and his caretaker, Lily, from the airport just the day before and were in great spirits. They were coming to spend their vacation with us, and we were looking forward to it very much. Sedrick was so happy that Saturday morning while driving to the airport. I glanced at him and saw him singing along to some of his favorite music in the car. After picking them up, we stopped and ate lunch at the Spring Garden Cafe, a popular seafood restaurant we liked. It was a great meal, and we shared a lot of laughter and good conversation. Once we arrived home, my dad and Lily went to their rooms and settled in. Later, we enjoyed a relaxing evening sitting outside on the upstairs veranda. Afterward, we came downstairs to watch some television. I had even decorated the house for Christmas before they came so I wouldn't have to put up the decorations while they were there and take time away from their visit. I remember that evening, Sedrick asked me to turn on the Christmas tree because he wanted to see how it looked lit up, even though it was still only November. Little did I know then that it would be the last time he would ever see the Christmas tree.

    It was Dad and Lily's third trip to visit us in Jamaica. The first two visits were fun, and they both enjoyed themselves being there. Dad was so happy that he would have somewhere nice to spend a little time away from winter in Canada. Lily had been working for Dad for about ten years as a housekeeper. During the last few years, he had become a bit frail, so she also drove him to his medical appointments so that he wouldn't have to take a bus. Before his third wife Nadina passed away from cancer in 2007, Lily promised her that she would help look after him. She enjoyed working for Dad, and he always treated her kindly. He did not like to travel alone anymore, and he had asked Lily to accompany him on all the trips to assist him.

They were both very impressed with our beautiful home, and Sedrick was very proud to show it to them. On their first two visits, we took them to see the famous seven-mile Negril Beach in the Parish of Westmoreland. We also took them to meet Sedrick's family in his hometown of Savanna-la-Mar, eighteen miles from Negril, and brought them on a few sightseeing excursions on the island. Lily is a big Bob Marley fan, and she bought many Bob Marley souvenirs. On this trip, we had promised to bring Lily and Dad to the Bob Marley Museum in Kingston.

That Sunday at 2:30 a.m., I heard some dogs barking very loudly close by, and I got up to look out the bathroom window to see if anyone was around. It was very dark outside. There was no street light on the electric pole, and I couldn't see anyone. For some reason, Sedrick and I were wide awake by 4:00 a.m., and neither of us could fall back to sleep. After talking for a few minutes in bed, we both got up. I headed into the ensuite bathroom to get ready for the day ahead while Sedrick decided to check a few emails on the laptop computer. Everything started very routinely that morning.

I was downstairs in the kitchen around 6:45, preparing food for our dog and a family of stray cats. When Sedrick came downstairs, I handed him a Boost Nutritional Drink and asked him if he would bring it upstairs to Dad. He smiled and cheerfully took it upstairs, and I could hear the two of them in Dad's room for a few minutes chatting and sharing a chuckle about something. After Sedrick returned downstairs, we went outside together in the front yard to feed the animals. When they finished eating, we went inside and locked the front door. There were metal burglar bars that went around the perimeter of the entire front porch, but Sedrick did not bother to lock them with the padlock since we would be going back outside in a few minutes with water for the animals. Not locking up the burglar bars would prove to be a fatal mistake.

It was just after 7:00 a.m., and we were washing the food bowls in the laundry room sink. Suddenly, our dog Sandy started barking as though she was scared. Immediately, we dropped what we were doing to go and see why she was barking, but we were about to get the shock of our lives.

Sedrick and I stood frozen in the doorway; Sandy's frantic barking pierced the morning air, sending shivers down my spine. My heart raced, and a knot tightened in my stomach, a premonition of impending danger. The once familiar sounds of the morning now felt ominous, the cheerful chirping of birds now a stark contrast to the tension that hung thick in the air.

With each bark, Sandy's distress echoed through the house, amplifying the sense of urgency that enveloped us. I glanced at Sedrick, his expression mirroring my own unease, his eyes wide with fear and uncertainty. At that moment, time seemed to stand still, the weight of the unknown pressing down on us like a heavy blanket.

We approached Sandy, and her frantic movements only intensified, her eyes darting wildly as if trying to convey a warning that we couldn't quite grasp. My hands trembled as I reached out to soothe her, the warmth of her fur a stark contrast to the chill that ran down my spine.

The air hung heavy with anticipation, every loud tick of the wall clock in the kitchen, every rustle of the leaves outside, amplifying the sense of foreboding that gripped us. In the silence that followed Sandy's barks, a sense of dread settled over us like a suffocating fog, choking off any semblance of normalcy.

To our horror and absolute dismay, we could see two masked men wearing hoodies standing on our front porch. I am five-foot-six tall, and they looked around my height, or maybe an inch or two taller. One of the men was wearing an orange hoodie, and the other, a grey hoodie. Judging by their stature and clothing style, they seemed to be very young men. All I could say to Sedrick was, "Oh, my God!" We stood there, glued to the spot, feeling helpless. Neither of us seemed to know what to do. It felt like I was watching a scary movie, except it was real life. They tried to kick in our stained-glass front door but were unable to. They had now turned their attention to a side door on the porch that opened into the living room. Within seconds, they managed to kick the door in and were now inside our house. My poor Sedrick, not armed with anything to defend himself with, started to walk towards them. I think he was in complete shock, and so was I. We had kept a machete in the kitchen under the sink, but neither of us even remembered it was there. If he had grabbed it, he might have had a fighting chance and could have tried to cut them with it as they were breaking in. Perhaps he thought he could try to talk them out of their evil plan because I heard him ask, "Why are you doing this to us?" These would be the last words I ever heard him speak. They never even answered him but surrounded us very quickly. The one man wearing the orange hoodie was now pointing a gun at Sedrick, and the other one was holding a knife and had his back turned to me. I started thinking about Dad and Lily, who were upstairs and knew we were all in imminent danger. My heart sank, and I was so afraid.

The tension mounted, and the gravity of the situation sank in; waves of fear crashed over me, threatening to overwhelm every fiber of my being. The sight of those masked figures shrouded in anonymity sent shivers down my spine, leaving me paralyzed with dread. My heart raced erratically, each beat a drumming reminder of the peril we faced.

In that surreal moment, time seemed to stretch endlessly, elongating every breath, every heartbeat, into an eternity of uncertainty. My mind, a whirlwind of panic and desperation, grasped for a semblance of control, a flicker of hope amidst the encroaching darkness.

The man in the grey hoodie stood a couple of feet from me in the dining room. Suddenly, I looked over and realized my cell phone was on a little console table at the foot of the stairs, which was very unusual because I always left it in the kitchen whenever I came downstairs. Immediately, I went over, grabbed it, and started running up the stairs. If I could lock myself in the bedroom, I could phone the police and get help for all of us. I had never run so fast in my entire life. It was almost as though someone was pushing me up the stairs. I was wearing flip-flops and worried that I would trip on the stairs. As I reached the first landing, I glanced over and saw the gunman staring at me. He looked so scary with his orange hoodie and purple and silver mask. I thought that it looked like a carnival mask. The only part of his face showing were his eyes; I could see pure hatred, rage, and evil in them. It was funny because I thought those eyes looked very familiar, and it suddenly dawned on me that these two guys were probably people we knew! Luckily, he didn't shoot at me as I was running up the stairs. Maybe he wasn't expecting me to run, which may have surprised him. I was so scared for Sedrick and wished that I could have done something to help him.

Once I entered our bedroom, I quickly locked the door behind me. I heard footsteps pounding up the stairs and saw the doorknob turning. For an instant, I thought that Sedrick managed to get away from the gunman, and I was about to open the door.

Suddenly, in my head, I heard a loud voice saying, "Donna, DO NOT open that door!" I believe that my guardian angel was speaking to me, and I was glad that I listened because if I had opened that door, I would have been dead. Immediately after I heard this voice, I saw the bedroom door getting kicked in. My heart was racing, and I wondered if I was going to have a heart attack from fear. Somehow, I pressed the police emergency number with trembling fingers and ran into the main bathroom. I locked the bathroom door, ran into the enclosed toilet room, and locked that door. A police dispatcher finally came on the line. I frantically explained to her that two masked men had broken into our home and that one of them was holding my husband at gunpoint downstairs while the other one was armed with a knife and was kicking in the bedroom door upstairs. I spoke loudly on the phone, hoping that the guy at the bedroom door would hear me talking to the police, and I prayed they would leave and run away. Hopefully, he would not come any further once he realized there were more locked doors. I was terrified and thought that I was about to die, and I was shaking like a leaf. I only imagined what he was going to do to me with the knife. Now, I was also frightened about what was happening downstairs to Sedrick and what would happen to Dad and Lily if they found out we had guests. I was helpless to do anything more to help us and could only pray. The police seemed to be taking forever, and I called them back two more times, asking the dispatcher if they were coming. Again, I stressed the urgency of the situation to her. She told me that the police had gone to the wrong house.

All of a sudden, I heard a loud explosion and knew right away that it was a gunshot. Afterward, there was just dead silence in the house. I didn't hear one sound, and it was so eerily quiet. I unlocked the door, left the toilet room, and went to the bathroom window. Standing there, I started calling Sedrick's name over and over. There was no response from him. I was hoping that he had gotten away from the gunman and had run to a neighbor's house for help. However, I had a sick feeling in my stomach that something was wrong. Then, I started yelling out the window for help. I looked and could see Lily standing in the window in her bedroom. I asked her if she and Dad were all right, and she told me that she had run over to Dad's room, locked his door, and then locked herself into her bedroom when she heard the commotion downstairs. Some relief washed over me once I knew they were both all right. I was still calling Sedrick's name but got no answer.

A knot formed in the pit of my stomach, tightening with each passing moment as dread coiled around my senses like a viper ready to strike. Hope warred with despair, a tumultuous storm raging within me, as I clung to the fragile possibility that

Sedrick had escaped unscathed, seeking refuge in the safety of a neighbor's home.

Yet, despite my fervent prayers, a sense of foreboding gnawed at the edges of my consciousness, whispering sinister truths that I dared not acknowledge. With every fiber of my being, I yearned for a glimmer of hope amidst the darkness that threatened to consume me whole.

Two neighbors who lived up the street had also heard the gunshot and were coming down the road to see what had happened. I called them through the window and told them what had happened. They could see that the side door leading into the living room was wide open, and they walked back to their homes because they weren't sure whether the two men were still inside the house. I stood there debating whether or not I should come out of the bathroom and go downstairs to check on Sedrick, but something was telling me to stay inside until the police arrived.

After about half an hour, I saw a police car arriving with one policeman, who withdrew his firearm and instructed me to wait upstairs in the bathroom until he checked the premises. After everything was clear, he told me to come down. However, nothing could have prepared me for what I would see when I left the bathroom and went downstairs.

Life Interrupted

Chapter 2
My Beautiful Husband Shot

I knew that the dead don't breathe or move, but I never knew I would have to witness someone dead that could never be dead to me.

The first thing I saw was the destruction of the bedroom door. Only a section of the top of the door remained intact, and splintered pieces of wood were across the floor. This man had been in a frenzy of rage in his attempt to reach me. Even though he was small in stature like the other man, they were both wiry and strong. It terrified me to know just how badly he had wanted to kill me, and it chilled me to the bone. I looked at the desk upstairs and noticed they had stolen our Toshiba laptop computer.

I stood there amidst the wreckage of what was once our haven; a whirlwind of emotions threatened to consume me. Anger, sorrow, and helplessness mingled together, forming a storm that raged within the confines of my mind. But above all else, there was a profound sense of unease, a gnawing fear that lingered like a shadow, reminding me that nowhere was truly safe anymore.

With absolute dread, I made my way down the stairs. I was still shaking badly, and my legs felt like rubber. A very gory scene awaited me as I reached the bottom of the stairs. Sedrick was sitting on the sofa with his head slumped over the armrest, face down. He was still wearing one of his slippers. The other one had come off his foot. Bright red blood was dripping from his head and pooling rapidly on the sofa and the floor underneath him. The gunman had shot him in the head at close range. I was reeling with shock as I tried to compose myself, but I never fainted or threw up. It was the first time I had ever seen anything so horrific, and knowing that it was my husband magnified the intensity of it all tenfold. In a small voice, I asked the detective to check and see if he was still alive, even though it was apparent that he was gone. He felt the pulse on the side of his neck, then shook his head and said, "I'm afraid he is deceased." Next, I heard him call for a homicide unit to come to the house immediately. When I heard those words, I was in utter disbelief that this beautiful man that I had married was dead. I kept wishing that I was having a nightmare and that I would wake up at any moment.

Sedrick was only 55 years old, had always taken such good care of himself, and looked very young for his age. He ate a very healthy diet and exercise regularly, and I always thought he would live a long life like his parents. I wanted to grow old together in our lovely home. We had been standing at the laundry room sink, planning our day just a few minutes before this. Now, he had been stolen from me, just like that, by these two wicked men. They did not have the right to break in and destroy the sanctity of our home.

I felt like a part of me had died right there with my beloved Sedrick, and at that moment, I thought I could never live without him. Looking at him, I realized that I never even got the chance to say goodbye to him or tell him how much I loved him before he died. Never again would I get to hug him or hold his hand. I would never see his beautiful smile or hear his laughter or voice anymore. I could not even go over to him because I could disturb any potential evidence. Just imagine, the last face he saw before he died was his killer's face, instead of mine or any of the faces of his dear family beside him. These thoughts bombarded me, and I could not believe my whole world had just come crashing down.

The shock of Sedrick's sudden departure coursed through every fiber of my being, leaving me reeling in disbelief. How could someone so full of life be snatched away in an instant? The injustice of it all seared through my soul, igniting a fierce rage against the perpetrators who had callously shattered our world. How I wished we had lasted a little longer. How I wished that I had held him a little tighter and whispered those three simple words that now seemed so inadequate in the face of such profound loss. But time, relentless in its passage, had slipped through our fingers like grains of sand, leaving only the bitter taste of unfinished conversations and unspoken farewells.

The other thing that was so horrifying about the whole scene was the stark contrast between the beautiful Christmas tree and decorations and Sedrick's lifeless body just a few feet away. There was a cute little snowman on the table beside the front door holding a little red bucket that said, "Welcome friends" on it. From that point on, Christmas was spoiled. I felt weak and started to sob uncontrollably. It was the worst possible day of my life, and I felt like I couldn't bear it. I wondered why they didn't steal whatever they wanted and leave us alone. Material objects are replaceable, but not life, which is so sacred. I felt so violated and helpless.

My next thought was that I had to go upstairs and tell Lily and my dad what had happened to Sedrick. I did not know how I would have the strength. My dad, who had fallen back to sleep in his room after talking with Sedrick, had been awoken by all the commotion and the loud explosion. He was now coming out of his room to see what was going on, and I gently took him by the hand and led him back to his room. I got him to sit down, and all I could say was, "Dad, something terrible has happened." Lily was now in the room with us, and we looked at each other, both trying to hold back tears. Dad suddenly stood up and insisted that he wanted to know what had happened, but he was elderly, and we worried that the stress would be too much for him.

Eventually, I told him Sedrick had gotten shot, and he asked if he had died. All I could manage to do was nod my head, crying and telling them both how sorry I was. I felt so terrible that they had come for a vacation getaway and instead ended up almost losing their lives.

The anguish in their eyes mirrored my own, amplifying the ache in my heart. In their eyes, I saw the reflection of my own anguish—the silent plea for understanding, for absolution. It was a burden that I bore alone, a burden that threatened to consume me from within.

Dad started to walk out of the room and wanted to go downstairs to see his son-in-law.

I tried to hold him back, telling him that he didn't want to see Sedrick in this terrible condition, but he became angry and insisted that he wanted to see him. I think that my dad wanted to say goodbye to him in his way. My father was an army veteran who had seen many horrific things when he was in Europe during World War II, so he must have figured that he could deal with this. Finally, Lily and I let him go to see Sedrick, but I knew he was taking it very hard. He had loved him like he was his son. I could see the sorrow and shock on his face, and he looked so pale. Lily and I offered to make him a cup of coffee and told him to go and sit in his room. He told me how sorry he was that Sedrick was dead. The trauma that Dad experienced that day would come to affect his health badly.

We had never even gotten to have breakfast that morning. Even though food was the farthest thing from my mind, I made some toast because I felt like I might faint. I figured that we had all better try to eat something to try and keep our strength up before the rest of the police arrived. However, when I tried to eat the toast, I might as well have been eating cardboard. It was all I could do to force down a few bites, and I felt like I was choking. I could not eat after being through something so horrifying. The three of us went upstairs and sat on the veranda where we had all just been sitting the evening before with Sedrick and having a great time. Now, we all felt numb and not sure what to do. We were also still scared that the two killers could come back again. I asked Dad and Lily if they wanted to go back home right away or if they wanted to stay at a hotel. Dad insisted they remain at the house because this was where everything had taken place, and they needed to be there. He knew the police would be conducting their investigation, and we could not go anywhere. We would have to sit there and wait for the crime scene unit to arrive.

The toast lay forgotten, a grim reminder of the mundane rituals that now seemed inconsequential in the wake of tragedy. Its taste, once familiar and comforting, now felt foreign—alien to the numbness that gripped my senses. The thought of sustenance seemed futile, a futile attempt to stave off the relentless tide of despair that threatened to engulf us. Sitting there, surrounded by the remnants of shattered dreams, we grappled with the enormity of what had transpired.

I called Sedrick's brother Donald in his hometown of Savanna-la-Mar in Westmoreland and gave him the horrible news. He was crying on the phone and telling his sister Gloria what had happened to Sedrick, and I could hear her wailing. He told me he would drive up that afternoon with his brother Joseph, his nephew James, and Lloyd, a close family friend. I felt relieved that the three of us wouldn't have to stay by ourselves and was also thankful that nothing had happened to Dad or Lily. It made me shudder to think what would have happened if they had been downstairs when the killers came in. Maybe they also would have been killed right there on the spot. If I had gotten killed, I am very sure that my dad would have probably had a heart attack or a stroke. I think that the shock would have been too much for him if something had happened to me, his beloved daughter.

Chapter 3
Our Home, Now A Major Crime Scene

My home was now a crime scene; the home I had built lay mangled in the stench of blood, a horror show, misery personified.

Within the next half hour, our house, once our dream home, had become a major crime scene. A couple of neighbors had come in through the front door, and the lead detective yelled at them to get out because they were disturbing the crime scene. Police officers were all over the yard, on the street, and inside the house. One of them was standing on the road holding a large automatic rifle. Two other officers were standing on the road talking, and I overheard one of them say, "What a shame. He left that poor girl here in Jamaica all alone!" Other police officers were putting yellow crime scene tape across the road, and many neighbors had started gathering to stand vigil in front of the house. A police photographer had also arrived and began taking pictures of the front of our home. A local television news reporter was talking to a few people on the street.

The day became fittingly overcast and very gloomy. I could see three vultures circling over the house because they could smell death. They gave me the creeps, and I wanted them to go away.

There was a coroner's van from one of the funeral homes parked down the street, waiting to take my dear Sedrick away. I was in denial. I was trying to tell myself the van was not there for him, but a cold, hard reality was setting in.

The presence of law enforcement only served to amplify the magnitude of our devastation. Their sincere faces mirrored my own internal chaos, their urgent movements a stark reminder of the irrevocable truth we were forced to confront.

The words of the officers exchanged in hushed tones, pierced through the air like shards of glass, each syllable a painful reminder of the shattered future that lay before me. Their speculation only fueled the ache in my heart, a relentless reminder of the gaping void left by Sedrick's absence.

Amidst the flurry of activity, a sense of isolation engulfed me, like a lone ship adrift in a sea of sorrow. The gaze of curious onlookers bore down upon me; their murmurs served only to deepen my sense of seclusion.

A forensics team came inside wearing white sterile jumpsuits and booties to start processing the scene. Three detectives accompanied them and said they wanted to start the interview with Lily and me so they could find out what had happened. Lily and I came down to the kitchen to meet with them, and I told Dad to stay on the veranda where he could get some fresh air. At his age, I didn't want to have him put through the added stress of a police interview. He had already been through too much.

As we came downstairs, I could see the forensic team around Sedrick and the pool of blood on the floor, and the sofa was growing bigger and bigger. The whole scene looked grisly, and I felt so sad that my husband had to die in such a horrible way. There were signs that he must have put up quite a bit of a struggle. As a result of his fighting, the dining room china cabinet had gotten pushed sideways, and one of the stereo speakers in the living room had toppled over. There was also a bloody handprint on one of the decorative white columns that led into the living room. I started thinking about the fear Sedrick must have gone through before he had gotten shot and wondered what his final thoughts were. I'm sure he must have thought we were all going to die.

He died a hero, trying to do what he could to save us, and he would never know that Dad, Lily, and I had all survived. He had faced the horrors of that morning with courage and selflessness, his every action a testimony to his love for us. He had fought not for himself but for our safety, our survival. And though he would never know the outcome, never know that we had escaped the same fate that had claimed him, his heroism would live on in our memories, a beacon of light in the darkness of my grief.

The next few hours were grueling as the detectives questioned Lily and me about what happened. I felt so sorry that poor Lily had to become a part of this tragedy, and I knew how traumatized she must have been. She got caught in the middle, and she had nothing to do with the break-in and murder. There was a nagging feeling I had about who may have wanted us dead, and I gave some pertinent information to the detective who was questioning me that I thought might assist with the case. He wrote down everything I was telling him on his notepad while the other detective, who talked to Lily, also took a lot of notes. As I continued to answer an endless barrage of questions, I noticed that a boat from the Beaches Resort had just brought some tourists to the coral reef to go scuba diving. Ironically, it was from the same resort that Sedrick had just brought tourists to from the Montego Bay Airport on his last trip for JUTA Tours. Watching them through the kitchen window, I thought the scene was surreal. Here I was, speaking to a detective about his murder while all of these tourists were getting into the water and enjoying themselves. They were oblivious to the horrific events that had just taken place in this house, just a short distance away from them. I could not help but wonder what they would have thought if they only knew what had happened here.

After several hours, a forensics team member came into the kitchen and told me they would remove Sedrick from the sofa. His body had stiffened so much from being in a sitting position for so long that they could not lie him down flat on the gurney. They had to use a lot of physical force and broke his spine in the process, which only added to my distress. I knew that he could not feel it, but it seemed like one further indignity to his body, and it gave me a sickening feeling that I will never forget. My dad told me later on that he had watched from upstairs while the police were removing his body from the sofa and carrying him out of the house on the gurney. I felt so upset that he had to see all of that and that he was going through this nightmare.

Before the coroner's van took him away, the same man from the forensics team brought me the items that Sedrick had in his shorts pockets, which included his wallet and keys for the car and the bus. Pitifully, I started to cry as I clung to his possessions. Who would want to hurt such a nice man? Why did the gunman have to shoot him in the head? Even if he had been shot and permanently injured, I would have been so happy if he would have survived. Their evil plan was to come and kill us, and Sedrick had gotten killed in cold blood. The gunman made sure of it when he took the kill shot, and it seemed like it was something very personal.

The responding officer, Detective Steele, was the lead investigating officer. He gave me the horrible details of what happened to Sedrick. It appeared that he had started to struggle with the two men to give me time to run upstairs. The man with the knife had slashed Sedrick across the forehead before he ran upstairs after me. The forensics team had found blood on the floor upstairs. After DNA testing, it would turn out to be Sedrick's blood. After he got cut, his forehead was bleeding, and he had put his hand up to his face as he staggered weakly into the living room. The bloody handprint on the column in the living room was also his.

The gunman had followed him into the living room, and it was not clear whether Sedrick had sat down on the sofa or had gotten pushed. He then shot him at close range over the left eye. I asked the detective whether Sedrick would have still been alive after the shot, but he told me that he died instantly. He went on to explain to me that when a person gets shot in the head, they bleed from their ears, nose, eyes, and mouth. I had never seen so much blood in my whole life. It looked like a slaughterhouse in our living room.

The detective told me they had been searching for the bullet fragment inside the sofa but had not yet found it. I asked him if this was a robbery gone wrong, and he told me that he did not feel that robbery was the motive. The only thing missing from the house was the laptop computer. He said that if robbery had been the motive, other houses in the area would have gotten targeted also. Only our home had been broken into, which was very telling.

He also informed me that the man with the knife would have continued to kick down the other two doors upstairs until he got to me. Just as I had thought, it appeared that he stopped because the gunman had shot Sedrick, and now they knew they would have to make their getaway. The loud gunshot would have attracted the attention of neighbors right away. To know that the only reason I was still alive was because Sedrick had gotten shot was almost too much for me to bear.

The detective's words painted a vivid picture of the chaos that had unfolded that morning. The abruptness of the gunshot, the suddenness of Sedrick's fall, echoed in my mind like a haunting refrain. The stark reality that his injury had thwarted the intruders' plans filled me with a profound sense of sorrow.

To know that the trajectory of my life had been altered by a single bullet, by a single act of violence, left me reeling with a mixture of disbelief and resignation. The fragility of existence, the randomness of fate, seemed to hang over me like a shadow, casting doubt upon the certainty of tomorrow.

It appeared they had no idea we had guests since my dad and Lily had only arrived the day before. The detective said that he believed it was a setup and it was probably someone we knew who lived nearby. We had been going about our daily lives without any idea that someone had put a price on our heads. I wondered how long they had been plotting this deadly home invasion.

The other thing that floored me was when he told me they must have been watching us for quite some time, studying our routine. They knew we came outside at about the same time every morning to feed the animals. They had been hiding in the

Life Interrupted

bushes near our house in the dark that night, getting themselves ready. To know that we were all in our beds sleeping, and the men were right outside, just waiting to make their move, made me shudder. There were footprints on the top of the wall alongside the house where they had jumped over. It made me think they must have arrived when I heard the neighbor's dogs barking. If only I had seen something when I looked out the window, I could have prevented what had happened to us.

I felt like a foreigner in my own skin; I felt violated; how could I ever feel safe knowing that someone out there could so easily stalk me, that anyone at any moment could be watching me; this incident took from me being secured in my own skin, it felt that I would never be able to feel safe again.

Detective Steele assured me he and his team would do their best to solve the case and gave me his condolences. My mind was racing as I listened to him, and I could not wrap my mind around who would have wanted to harm us. Sedrick had every right to come back to his homeland to live. We were just two ordinary people who, through honest, hard work and saving up our money and a bank line of credit, had been fortunate enough to be able to build our dream home. All we wanted to do was live the peaceful life we had come here for. We had not asked for any of this.

Afterward, I asked the detective who had been interviewing me if they could get someone to clean up all the blood because I could not do it. He told me they don't clean up crime scenes and I would have to do it myself. I could see black fingerprint dust all over the house where the police were processing the scene for fingerprints. Suddenly, the house didn't feel like a home anymore but felt like a death trap. The three of us had seen terrible things that day that no human being should ever have to see.

Chapter 4
The Aftermath

Sometimes, they just won't let you forget it; they, everyone, doing grief's bidding.

Luckily, I had some kind neighbors, and a few of them volunteered to come into the house to clean up after the police left. The next thing I knew, they were grabbing buckets, rags, and bleach and started cleaning up all the blood on the floor and were trying their best to comfort us. I remember asking a couple of them to remove the bloody sofa because I never wanted to see it again. To try and take my mind off the horrible scene, I started sweeping the floors and washing off all the fingerprint dust.

As we cleaned up the mess from that awful day, the repetitive sounds of scrubbing and sweeping oddly felt like a way to escape. It was a bit of relief from the heavy, sad feeling that lingered around. My neighbors chatting and helping out gave a short break from the overwhelming emotions.

But, no matter how hard we cleaned, the memories and the pain just wouldn't go away. The reality of what happened stuck in my mind, and no amount of cleaning could make it disappear. Wiping away fingerprints and blood stains didn't change the fact that the emotional scars were still there, deep down.

Other neighbors came into the yard, hugged me, and gave me their sympathies. By now, Sedrick's two brothers, his nephew, and their family friend had arrived and were in the house with us. Lily decided to try to make something for all of us to eat. None of us had any appetite, but we had to try and keep our strength up. It had been the worst day of our lives, and we were all so distraught. As we sat down to eat, it felt weird. How could we even think about food when this heavy, gut-wrenching feeling was tearing us apart inside? The reality that someone we loved had been taken away from us, and a part of us had gone with him, made it hard to swallow anything. Eating seemed so trivial compared to the gaping hole in our hearts. But we tried, not because we wanted to, but because we had to, even if it felt like an impossible task. The pain inside us was just too big to ignore, and it overshadowed everything, including the food on our plates.

The phone started ringing off the hook because other members of Sedrick's family had gotten the horrible news, and everyone was calling me, wanting to know the details of what had taken place. It was so difficult for me to talk to them about it without bursting into tears, and so very hard for any of us to comprehend why this had happened to us.

Every time I had to tell them, it felt like ripping open the wound again. It was tough for me to talk about it without breaking down, and for all of us, it was just impossible to wrap our heads around why this had hit us so hard.

Each time the phone rang, and I had to go through the details again, it felt like reliving the whole thing. Explaining what went down brought back the same emotions, making me feel like I was right there in that terrible moment once more. It was like a brutal cycle – someone calls, I recount the story, and the pain hits me all over again. Talking about it was a constant reminder of the heartbreaking incident, and it made the hurt fresh every single time.

I also discovered that the story was all over the local television news, but we didn't want to watch the newscast. Days later, I finally got the nerve to watch the news report online, and it hurt to see it. Seeing our story on the news made everything so real, yet it felt unreal at the same time. We've all watched the news before, right? Never thought it would be about us one day. It's like you never see it coming until it hits you square in the face. We never knew our lives would end up on the news, but I guess life throws curveballs when you least expect it.

That evening, Dad, Lily, and I tried to find something funny on television to watch to have a little distraction, and it was a relief that there were other people in the house with us.

I asked Lily if I could come and sleep in her room because I never wanted to sleep in our bedroom again. Neither of us could sleep much, and we started talking about what had happened. Lily told me that when she heard the commotion, she had peeked from upstairs and heard Sedrick speaking to the two killers in the dining room. The gunman had glanced up and seen her. She then ran and locked my dad's bedroom door and locked herself into her bedroom. Then she leaned against the wall and prayed, "Oh, Dear God, this can't be happening!"

I could not believe I would no longer be sleeping beside my husband after all those years. I never saw it coming, you know? That sudden stop to our connection was just unbearable. I never realized I'd never have him sleeping next to me again. It's like life pulled the rug from under us, and the shock of it made everything feel so raw. The idea that our shared nights were suddenly gone, it was just too much to wrap my head around.

That very night, I had a horrible nightmare that someone was chasing me around in the house and trying to shoot me. I woke up after this bad dream, and I was shaking.

I couldn't shake this guilt that hung over me because I made it out, but Sedrick didn't. I heard about survivor guilt, but now it was hitting me hard. Questions started swirling in my head – could I have done something different? Maybe if I stayed downstairs, tried talking to those two guys, could I have helped Sedrick?

It's like this heavy feeling that you don't deserve to be okay when someone close to you isn't. Surviving feels like a double-edged sword – relief on one side, guilt on the other. I kept thinking about all the "what ifs" and wondering if my actions could've changed things. It's tough, feeling like maybe there was something more I could've done to change the outcome. Survivor guilt messes with your mind, makes you question everything.

I wished that things could have turned out differently and that he could have saved himself. How could he fight off two armed men when he had nothing to defend himself with? A few months prior, he had talked to me about purchasing a legal firearm for protection, and quite a few of the tour bus drivers in Jamaica do carry one in case someone tries to rob them. I felt so bad because I told him that I was scared of guns and was uncomfortable having one in the house. Now, I have come to regret this decision very much. Maybe there would have been a different outcome, and it would have been one of the killers dead instead of him if I had just let him go ahead and get a gun. I remember the detective telling me that if Sedrick had shot one of them, he never would have been charged because he was defending his home and family. These thoughts haunted me for the rest of the night, and I felt horrible in the morning.

When I came downstairs in the morning, Lily was already in the kitchen preparing breakfast for all of us. I was so thankful to have her in the house with me to help out. She was such a Godsend, and I don't know how I would have managed to be able to cook when I was so overwhelmed by everything that had happened. I kept thinking how brave she was to want to stay there after what had happened, and I felt so bad for what she had to endure.

Suddenly, I panicked because I thought that if these killers took the computer, they might try to see if they could hack into our bank account online. I decided I needed to go to the bank in Ocho Rios immediately to report it to be on the safe side. No one had told me I should do this; it had just occurred to me. I was surprised that considering everything that had happened, at least a part of my brain was still functioning.

It's strange, you know? In the midst of all the pain and chaos, your mind kind of goes numb. But then there are moments, like this one, where you're suddenly hyper-aware. Was it alertness or just sheer dread? I questioned what else I could lose, and that fear pushed me to take action. It's like my brain, despite being overwhelmed, found a way to kick into gear when it mattered most.

As I went downtown and started walking to the bank, I could see and hear people passing by all around me, but I felt like a complete zombie. I could hardly even feel my feet touching the ground, and I felt like I was moving slowly in a daze. It was uncanny to see everything around me looking normal, but for me, nothing would ever be normal again. It's like standing in the same spot but feeling like you've stepped into a whole different dimension. Everyone else was going about their lives, but mine felt completely upside down. It's this surreal feeling, like you're living in a parallel universe, and even though you're surrounded by the usual sights and sounds, your whole existence is just on a different wavelength. Sedrick and I walked on the same street that Friday morning, conducting our daily business, and he was smiling and talking with one of the tellers at the bank. Later that day, he went to Sangster International Airport to pick up some tourists and came home happy because he had received great tips. The once beautiful, idyllic life that I knew was turned upside down. I had become an unwilling participant in my own horror story. Every spot that Sedrick and I had been to turned into a stark reminder of what I had lost – not just him, but a chunk of who I was. It was like a heavy cloud hanging over every place, soaking it with memories that felt bittersweet – they were all stamped with his absence.

Each place echoed with what used to be, and it hit me right in the gut. It wasn't just bricks and mortar; it was a collection of moments, laughter, and shared experiences that now felt like ghosts haunting every corner. It's strange how the familiar can transform into a painful reminder, making me long for the times when those spots were filled with warmth and joy.

Life Interrupted

Now, it's like they're frozen in time, forever tied to the person I lost and the part of me that went with him.

When I finally reached the bank, I asked to speak to the manager, who was very helpful.

She cancelled our joint debit cards, issued me a new one, and expressed her condolences when she heard my story. Some of the tellers who knew Sedrick were shocked by the sad news. The manager brought out his file and wrote "deceased" across the front. I couldn't believe I had to see that word next to his picture, and it just didn't feel real to me. Everything was reminding me of his sudden absence, and each time it was shocking me the same. I guess, the reality hits really hard, but doesn't embed itself easily. At least no one would be able to get access to our bank accounts, which gave me a bit of relief.

I was seeking relief anywhere I could find, but the truth is that I would have given everything to have him back. I thanked the manager for her assistance and compassion, and she wished me all the best.

All the best... each word was an empty casket to me. What best could possibly come after what I had just been through? I know they meant well...

The next day, a few of the neighbors came over with a pastor from one of the local churches to have a prayer session with us to try and give us all some much-needed spiritual comfort. We had a few more prayer meetings with different pastors from other churches over the next few days. One morning, a Baptist minister came in and put his hand on my shoulder as he started to pray. All of a sudden, he was so overcome by our grief and the brutality of what had happened that he broke down sobbing and could not even continue. He asked one of his church sisters to continue the prayer, and he just sat there, overcome by his emotions. It touched me deeply, and I also cried. Also, the chaplain from the Police Chaplaincy Services Branch came to give his condolences and handed me a pamphlet on the seven stages of grieving. I glanced at it and realized that I was in the first stage of grieving, which is shock and denial.

Just a few days after the murder, the lead detective called me one afternoon to inform me that I would need to go to the morgue at the Kingston Public Hospital by 8:30 a.m. the next day to make an identification of my husband's body. I was surprised by this since I had already identified him at the house the day of the murder. A pathologist was going to be performing an autopsy on his body. My stomach started to feel very queasy again just thinking about it. I had never had to go to a morgue before, and I wondered how I would get through this. Again, I could not get to sleep that night. I kept picturing his lifeless body in front of me, like he's there but not really there. It's this haunting image that reminds me of who I lost, who got taken away from me. The whole thing felt unreal, like I was caught in this nightmare that just wouldn't end.

That morning, I got ready to head out early with Sedrick's brother Joseph and their family friend Lloyd to beat the traffic since it was a long drive. I had asked Gwen, a neighbor that lived up the street, whether Dad and Lily could come and spend the day at her house while we were gone. She kindly welcomed them into her home, and I was very grateful. On the way to the Kingston Public Hospital, I sat in the back seat in tears. I didn't know how I was going to be able to go to this awful place. I brought a beautiful photo of Sedrick in my purse and intended to take it out and look at it right after I identified him. It would be my coping mechanism.

Isn't it ironic? How a mere photo was now a coping mechanism for the reality? I could have never imagined him being near me as a dreadful sight, until it was...

We seemed to take forever to get to the hospital because rush hour traffic in the Spanish Town area was heavy and slow-moving. Finally, we arrived and made our way over to the morgue. As we went inside the waiting room, I was struck by how cold it was there, and I started to shiver. I also noticed there was a horrible stench of blood and death, and I knew I would never forget it. Each step I took in there was a count of how many times I felt horror. There was death in the air, cold and bloody.

A woman came in with blue overalls and rubber boots. She was responsible for cleaning up after the pathologist completed all the autopsies. Time felt like it was standing still as we sat there waiting for the pathologist to arrive to perform the autopsy.

Two other women came in, and they were both sobbing. I learned that they were sisters, and their mother had died in a traffic accident. They had come there to identify her body. I told them what had happened to my husband, and then we gave our condolences to each other. For those few brief minutes that we were all sitting in the waiting room together, we were all united in our grief and numbing pain. As I said, in moments like these, we all hurt the same. Grief is what brings us all together, despite the differences.

Detective Steele arrived a short time later, along with another police officer and a photographer. After he wrote down some information in a book, I saw them all putting on white jumpsuits and booties over their shoes, and they went inside the autopsy room. They went in to take pictures of the body and would be present for the autopsy. A few more excruciating minutes passed, the door opened, and the detective came out to tell me it was time to go in. My hands were sweating, and my knees felt weak and shaky, but I knew that I had no choice; I had to do this. I asked him if I could bring my brother-in-law in, and he told me that only one of us was permitted to go in. He asked me to go since I was the spouse, but he knew I was nervous and took me by the hand. I swallowed hard as he led me inside, and I felt sick in the stomach.

When I went into the room, there were five or six other bodies, all in white body bags. Then I saw Sedrick, and the pathologist was standing next to him. He never even asked me if I was ready before he made me see him. Sedrick was still inside the unzipped body bag. I could feel my heart skip a beat and was alarmed to see that he was still not cleaned up. When slumped over the sofa, I could not see the full extent of his wounds because he had been face-down into the armrest of the sofa bed. Now, the brutality of what he had endured was on full display. During the fight, the man slashed him across the forehead with the knife. The bullet, which had entered his head right above his left eyebrow, had shattered his eye, and his mouth was slightly open with dried blood all around it. Maybe he was saying a prayer before he got shot, or perhaps he was begging for his life. I'm not sure. When I saw him like this, it reminded me that he did not die a peaceful death but in abject fear. My husband, who was once so full of energy and life, was now lying here dead on this cold, steel autopsy table. He had been executed, killed in cold blood. The pathologist asked me my name and whether or not this was my husband, Sedrick Anthony. I managed to answer him, but I was sobbing. He never even offered his condolences or any words of comfort to me. I guess this was just all in a day's work to him. It was more than I could take, and I just ran from the room. The detective asked my brother-in-law Joseph to take me out of the environment.

We went outside to try and get some fresh air while we waited for the autopsy to be over. I took out the picture that I brought along and looked at it, and it was how I wanted to remember Sedrick, looking handsome with his dazzling smile. I tried hard to keep this image in my head and push away the awful scene that I had just witnessed inside the morgue.

A short time later, the detective came out, said the autopsy was over, and handed me a pink form. Both the pathologist and the detective had signed it, and it stated both the date and cause of death. It said that Sedrick had died from a gunshot wound to the head and a perforation to the brain. There it was in black and white! To see the cause of death in writing looked so graphic. I felt like my heart was ripped in two once again after I read it. I would have to bring this form to the Registrar's Office, have the death registered, and obtain the official Death Certificate.

His brother Joseph got the chance to go and see Sedrick alone following the autopsy, and I stayed outside and waited. When Joseph came out afterward, he was understandingly very emotional, and he expressed his anger over the murder.

Imagine what it must feel like to know that one of your siblings was a murder victim.

We waited for the arrival of another van that was going to transport his body from the morgue to a funeral home in his hometown of Savanna-la-Mar. It took quite a while, but the van from Doyley's Funeral Home finally arrived to take away our Sedrick.

Afterward, I wanted to go far away from this awful place and go home. It had been yet another gut-wrenching day. I made a vow to myself that I would see these hoodlums caught and put away in prison for the rest of their lives.

I started to worry about my dad, as he had developed a bad cough just a couple of days after the murder. It was making it hard for him to get a good night's sleep, and he said he wasn't feeling well. I called a doctor who lived in the neighborhood and asked her if she could come to the house and take a look at him. He had caught a bad cold due to all the trauma and stress, and she gave him a prescription cough medicine and told Lily and me to make sure he was getting some rest. After about a week, the cold seemed to improve, but Dad would never be the same again.

The whole ordeal took a heavy toll on all of us. Immediately following the murder, I developed symptoms of irritable bowel syndrome. I lost seventeen pounds rapidly, and my clothes no longer fit me properly. My lower back was hurting a lot, which I attributed to all the tension in my body. Lily had also lost weight, and I could see how stressed out she was. She confided to me that she hadn't even told her husband or family what had happened over the telephone, or they would have been too scared for her safety. She never told them until she went back to Ottawa.

Lily and Dad agreed to stay with me for about two more weeks. The original plan was that Lily would go home a few days before Christmas, and Dad would stay with Sedrick and me until New Year's Day.

After what happened, we hardly wanted to leave the house. The only time we would go out was when some neighbors brought us to the grocery store in Ocho Rios to buy food. Another day, we went out for lunch at the Spring Garden Cafe. It was the same seafood restaurant we had gone to with Sedrick the day we had picked Dad and Lily up from the airport. I told the waitress what had happened to him because we used to eat there frequently, and he knew most of the staff there. All the staff members were devastated when I gave them the awful news.

I got the same reaction whenever I went to any of the stores or businesses in Ocho Rios. Everyone who talked to Sedrick thought he was a wonderful, pleasant man and could not believe that someone would want to murder him. They all had the same opinion as me that the motive had to be jealousy. Time and time again, I heard many news stories about people who got killed in Jamaica because of it.

The day Dad and Lily left to go back home, I could see that Dad was very worried about me and hated leaving me there. It was written all over his face. I told them both how much I loved them, wished them a safe trip, and tearfully hugged them both before they reached the security gate at the airport. They would not be in Jamaica for the funeral, but I knew that it would be too much for them, especially Dad, and it would be safer for them to go home to Canada.

Chapter 5
Planning A Painful Farewell

Farewell, the irony.

The date for Sedrick's funeral was set for Saturday, December 14, 2013, just a little over a week before Christmas. In preparation for his burial in Savanna-la-Mar, I stayed at the family home. In Jamaica, it is customary for funerals to take place up to a month after a person dies. Many relatives live abroad in different countries, and this gives them the time they need to make travel arrangements. Other members of his family started to arrive from Ottawa, Toronto, Miami, and New York.

My sister-in-law Sheila had come from Toronto and was going to help me with all the funeral arrangements. We would have never dreamed it would be for Sedrick in a million years. His brother Donald, who was self-employed as a very talented carpenter, would be making the casket. It must have been a difficult and painful undertaking for him because he had always been very close to Sedrick all of their lives.

I remember the day that Sheila and I went to the funeral home to take care of the arrangements and make the down payment. As I was sitting there listening to her discussing the floral arrangements with the secretary, I felt myself being rather detached. I was in denial again, and I told myself that it couldn't possibly be my husband we were talking about, but it must be someone else. We went outside afterward to pick his final resting spot. Everything felt so unreal to me. I tried my best not to start crying because I felt so overwhelmed by my emotions.

Sitting at the funeral home amidst discussions of floral arrangements and final resting places, the world felt surreal, as if I was trapped in a nightmare from which I could not awaken. Denial wrapped its tendrils around my heart, shielding my fragile spirit from the full force of her grief. Yet, beneath the surface, emotions simmered, threatening to spill over at any moment. Denial can be very welcoming in moments of grief; it is very simple to give in, just shut that part, the reality of everything, but when is life that simple? When is truth that simple? I could not deny it; I wished I could, but sanity prevailed, grief prevailed.

Back at the house, a few of his siblings were reminiscing about their beloved brother, and the mood was somber. My brother-in-law's woodworking shop was at the back of the house, and to add to our pain, we had to see the unfinished casket there every day.

It was just another grim reminder of what had happened, and I could hardly bear to look at it.

After showing the brochure on grieving to Sedrick's family, I read that I was now in stage two, which is pain and guilt. It brought raw, unimaginable pain that seemed almost physical and excruciating. Instead of hiding it or avoiding it, I tried to experience the pain fully because it was the only way to work through it.

Once we had finished all the funeral arrangements, it was time to start thinking about writing the eulogy. I had brought a photo album of our wedding pictures to show the family, and I began to flip through it alone that evening. Several members of his family were writing about their precious memories of Sedrick, and I sat down to write mine. I thought about our life together and the stories I wanted to share about this wonderful, endearing man.

Donna M. McCully

Chapter 6
Our Love Story

Love was in the air, the world seemed beautiful enough to drown all sorrows.

We met while I was out Christmas shopping one late November day in 1984. I had just bought a set of dishes for my mother. The two boxes were heavy, and I was struggling to carry them on my way to catch a bus to go home to my apartment. Out of the blue, I heard a voice behind me asking me if I needed any help. When I turned around, this tall, very handsome man stood there smiling at me, and I thought he was gorgeous! His thoughtfulness touched me, so I let him carry one of the boxes for me. As we walked along, we started talking, and before long, he asked me if I would have time to go and have a coffee with him. I accepted the invitation. After we sat down with our coffees, we started getting to know each other. Just before he walked me to my bus stop, he asked me for my telephone number.

My heart raced with joy when he phoned and invited me out a few days later. I dashed off to buy a new dress, eager to dazzle him. Our first date fell on a Friday night, just before Christmas, and we ended up at Hartwell's, this bustling nightclub nestled in the Westin Hotel. As we danced, there was this undeniable spark, a magnetic pull between us. It felt like we'd known each other forever, like our souls had finally found their match. That night, I sensed something special blooming, a love so sweet and unexpected. It's a moment etched in my heart, one I'll cherish forever.

After a whirlwind romance, he proposed to me on Valentine's Day, 1985. There still weren't a lot of interracial marriages in the mid-eighties. A man that I worked with at the time was a bigot, and he told me that he could not condone the marriage. I didn't care what other people thought, and I just knew that I loved this man and wanted to spend the rest of my life with him. I accepted his proposal, and we decided to elope the following week. It was a cold and snowy evening on February 21, 1985, when we got married. Looking through all the photos, I could see how young we were and that we had our whole lives ahead of us. At the time, I had just turned 23 years old, and he was 26. I smiled to myself as I recalled the happiest day of my life. We loved being together and were like two peas in a pod. Our common interests included our mutual love of animals, music, movies, swimming, and exercising. We enjoyed dining out whenever we could. Sedrick and I always loved to dance and used to go out almost every weekend for the first few years we were married. Since we lived downtown at the time, we could walk to all the nightclubs, bars, theatres, and restaurants. Getting all dressed up and going out after a long work week was a great way to unwind and destress.

Sedrick cherished his family deeply, holding onto their connection through frequent phone calls despite their scattered locations across the world. Even amidst his affection for Canada, his heart remained tethered to his roots and cherished culture. Amidst the bustling University of Ottawa, a local radio station became our solace, serenading us with reggae tunes every Saturday morning as we tackled household chores together. Sedrick, with his culinary prowess, delighted me with his delectable Jamaican dishes, each bite a nostalgic journey. The New Year's Eve parties hosted by Sedrick's Jamaican friends were nothing short of magical. The air was thick with the aroma of flavorful Jamaican delicacies, laughter echoing in every corner. A DJ spun reggae melodies, beckoning us to dance until the early hours, our spirits soaring amidst the rhythm of the night.

We drove to Toronto on the first long weekend in August to attend Caribana, the largest Caribbean festival in North America. It was great to go and watch the colorful parade, visit his cousins and sister over the weekend, and go to the Metro Toronto Zoo.

The first time Sedrick brought me to Jamaica was in 1988, and I fell in love with the country. We spent our vacations at his family home and went back several times over the next few years. He said he always felt so good to come back home again. He'd always go and find his old friends from the neighborhood and reminisce with his sister and brother about childhood memories. I could still picture him laughing and joking around with them in the backyard or climbing the mango trees to pick his favorite mangoes. We loved to go swimming every day at Negril Beach, and we would also stay at one of the all-inclusive resorts for a couple of nights to have some time to ourselves away from the family. Our vacations to Jamaica were always relaxing and very romantic.

Sedrick's cherished niece, Angelica, resides in the vibrant city of New York, and we were fortunate enough to spend an entire week enveloped in her warm company. We immersed ourselves in the iconic landmarks that define the city's skyline, creating lasting memories against the backdrop of its bustling streets. Our adventures extended beyond the city limits, impulsively venturing to the sun-kissed shores of Puerto Vallarta, Mexico, and the picturesque landscapes of Prince Edward Island. The winding roads also beckoned us on spontaneous long weekend journeys to the enchanting destinations of Montreal, Quebec, and Kingston, Ontario. Amidst the varied landscapes and experiences, the true magic unfolded in the simple joy of being together, forging a bond that made each moment an unforgettable part of our shared journey.

We were happy and excited when we bought our first home together in 1992. We had been renting an apartment since we got married and were so proud to be able to buy our little condominium. It was a great accomplishment and a turning point for us to become homeowners.

He was a very vibrant man with a great personality and was outgoing, warm, and friendly. Wherever we went, he could make friends easily. Many staff members knew him by his first name in the restaurants or hotels we used to like to go to. He loved to talk to people, was very charming, and had a wonderful sense of humor.

I was so lucky that he was always there for me and was my shoulder to lean on. Sedrick was helpful around the house, and he also enjoyed doing volunteer work with me.

Simple things used to make him happy. One of our favorite things to do in summer was to go for long walks in the park. We would go and sit beside the pond and watch the ducks and geese. Sometimes, it was nice to sit and not even have to talk. Just being in each other's presence was comforting. It was almost as if we each knew what the other was thinking. When you're married for such a long time, you develop a strong bond with each other. He was a very thoughtful man who loved to surprise me with little gifts and always made me feel beautiful. I felt loved and protected around him, and we adored each other.

Even though Sedrick and I never experienced parenthood together, I have no doubt he would have been an extraordinary father, for his affection for children was unmistakable. In the presence of his young nieces, nephews, or any little ones, his countenance would radiate with warmth and tenderness. Reflecting on this, I believe that sharing a child with him could have provided solace amidst his departure, lessening the weight of solitude while preserving a part of him within our lives. The notion of adoption had crossed our minds on several occasions throughout our journey together, yet we grappled to find common ground on the matter. Regrettably, the dream of parenthood eluded us, and I've come to embrace the truth that certain paths simply aren't destined for us.

We were two souls in the universe brought together in wedded bliss. He was the perfect husband for me, and I couldn't have asked for a better man. Not only was he my life partner, but he was also my best friend and soulmate, and he had a heart of gold. We planned on renewing our wedding vows in Jamaica at our favorite resort, Sans Souci, for our 30th anniversary, which would have been so special.

Now, as I looked at our wedding photos and saw how handsome he looked in his tuxedo, I couldn't believe that after living in Jamaica for only fifteen months, he was gone from my life forever. I never thought that I would become a widow at this age.

Chapter 7
Ominous Warning Signs

We're all blind to red when it comes to love.

I began reflecting on a few warning signs we had received, and we should have listened, but now it was too late. You should stop and pay close attention when you feel someone or something is trying to tell you something.

In November 2012, we got our first sign that something was wrong just three months after we had moved in. We were asleep, and it was about 4:00 a.m. when we were startled awake by a loud bang at the back door. We both jumped out of bed, and Sedrick ran to flip on the lights in the house. Whoever was there had run away when they saw the lights come on. When it was daylight, we went outside to check and see the damage. Someone had tried to pry open one of the windows near the back door, and the door itself was damaged. There were metal burglar bars on the inside of the wooden door, so they were not able to get in. At the time, we had a couple of men working in the yard laying sod. That evening, they had left their pitchfork and two machetes outside instead of putting them away in the garage, and the pitchfork was lying on the back step. There were muddy footprints on the steps and some fingerprints on the window. We were both terrified and called the police. After the police arrived, they drew their weapons and checked the premises. I asked the Sergeant to take fingerprints, but they refused. The explanation that he gave me was that the sea air had distorted the fingerprints, rendering them unreadable. They should have taken them anyway.

Life Interrupted

Two nights later, it happened again, around 8:30 p.m. The TV flickered with light as another loud bang echoed through the house, jolting us from our evening calm. My heart pounded against my chest like a drumbeat as I rushed to the window, desperation fueling my voice as I yelled at whoever lurked beyond to leave us be. Looking back now, it felt like a silent warning, urging us to heed its message. Then, on another restless night, darkness enveloped our neighborhood in an eerie embrace, swallowing the comforting glow of streetlights. For hours, we sat in the gloom, grappling with fear's icy grip. As dawn broke, we ventured outside, only to find muddy footprints staining the porch once more. It marked the third ominous visit to our back door. Yet, despite our pleas for help, the authorities remained indifferent, leaving us to fend for ourselves in the shadows of uncertainty.

All they did was drive around and tell us to put more lights around the house outside.

I told Sedrick a few times afterward that I had a bad feeling they would come back again. We were both uneasy after that and sometimes heard strange little sounds in the yard at night. Some nights, the sea became quite rough, and the sound of the waves made it very hard to hear other noises. It made us sleep downstairs on the sofa bed in the living room frequently. We wanted to hear if anyone was trying to get in. One night, we both thought we heard someone running through the yard, and I think someone was there.

Funny, we did look at a couple of beautiful condominiums during the summer of 2013.

They lived in these safe, gated communities, wrapped in security round the clock, with stunning views of the sea. One of them even boasted a private beach. Imagine, there was this underground parking garage where Sedrick could have safely parked the bus. I'll never forget that moment on the condo balcony, gazing at the vista, seeing the spark in his eyes. He envisioned us there, happy as can be. We toyed with the idea of selling the house and making one of those condos our home. But something held us back, a feeling maybe, whispering that it wouldn't be easy to let go. Looking back, I realize it was a sign nudging us to move, and I deeply regret not listening. It's a shame, and I wish I had been more persuasive, tried harder to make him see.

Another odd incident occurred. On Easter weekend in April 2013, we decided to take a road trip to visit his sister and brother and stay for a night with them in Savanna-la-Mar. Sedrick and I sat down for breakfast around 6:00 a.m. on Good Friday. There was no more milk for our coffee, so Sedrick ran to the little shop two doors down to buy some. He had known the owner of the shop for many years. All of a sudden, I heard someone yelling, "Murder, murder!" and Sedrick came running back inside the house. People were now running up the road to see what the commotion was all about.

Sedrick was shook up as he told us what had happened. Just as he was about to enter the shop, he saw two well-dressed young men with gold chains standing outside. They were about to go in but seemed hesitant when they saw him. One of them was on his cell phone. Just seconds after Sedrick was coming out of the shop, they rushed in with guns drawn and robbed the man in the shop of all his gold rings! Maybe they thought Sedrick was a policeman because he was very clean-shaven and happened to be wearing navy blue cargo pants that day. He was lucky he avoided getting caught in the middle of the robbery, or maybe he could have gotten hurt or worse. That same day, he told his niece he would like to get a licensed firearm. In hindsight, I am so sorry that I never let him get one. It was another warning to us.

Since we got the bus back in July 2013, a wave of unease washed over me at the thought of leaving it out in the driveway. I must've brought it up to Sedrick a handful of times, suggesting he inquire at JUTA Tours if we could stash it in their lot rather than risk it at home. Sedrick fretted over the possibility of someone making off with the bus if it were parked elsewhere. Little did we know, that decision would haunt us. That fateful morning, as sunlight broke through, those perpetrators scaled the wall and huddled behind our bus, patiently awaiting our appearance to unlatch the burglar bars. Had it not been parked there, their sinister ploy would have been thwarted, and perhaps we could have glimpsed them lurking in the yard.

The final warning struck us hard in early September 2013. Sedrick had already invested in the bus and completed all the hoops to secure his JUTA membership and vehicle carrier license when the insurance bombshell dropped. Walking into the insurance office that morning, we were met with devastating news: Sedrick hadn't been driving in Jamaica long enough to operate the bus. It felt like a gut punch. The agent explained he'd need someone else to drive it. Sedrick's frustration was palpable; he felt blindsided, wishing they had mentioned this hurdle earlier.

We trudged from one insurance company to another, but each echoed the same rejection. Disheartened, Sedrick was ready to throw in the towel. He confided in me, his dream of making a living in Jamaica crumbling. It was the very reason we'd come here – to build a future. He proposed returning to Canada, but I reminded him of the bitter winters awaiting us there.

Defeated, we returned to the first insurance company, clinging to a sliver of hope. Little did we know, this would be the turning point, albeit a tragic one. The agent's words hung heavy in the air as she relayed the manager's discovery of a loophole. Relief washed over us as Sedrick was granted insurance, yet little did I know, it was a deal with fate I'd forever regret.

If not for that loophole, we might've sold the bus and our home, seeking refuge in Canada. Instead, I faced the heart-wrenching reality of burying the man I cherished.

When you lose someone you love, what's left of you is nothing but a piece of what you were, and a reminder of what you lost.

Chapter 8
Laying My Husband to Rest

The kind of rest that left me restless forever...

The night before the funeral was a traditional Jamaican wake at the house. The atmosphere buzzed with a mix of sorrow and nostalgia as Sedrick's childhood friends and relatives gathered to commemorate his life. Outside, the air was filled with the rich aroma of soup, and the clinking of glasses echoed through the night. Amidst the laughter and animated conversations, my heart carried the heavy weight of grief. I sought solace in a quiet corner, enveloped in the somber embrace of my thoughts.

As people approached to offer their condolences, their words became a bittersweet reminder of the tragedy that had befallen us. The murder lingered in the air, casting a shadow over the otherwise vibrant gathering, leaving me grappling with a profound sense of loss and disbelief. People kept asking if the police had caught anyone for Sedrick's murder, and I had to keep saying no. The bus we had bought together was just sitting in the driveway at home, and whenever I looked at it, I couldn't help but imagine Sedrick driving it. It made me feel really alone. I didn't want it around because it reminded me too much of what we had planned. The bus would stay there until I could figure out the paperwork and sell it. Dealing with it was tough, like facing a constant reminder of the dreams we had that would never come true.

You're never prepared for this you know. You sit there blank, because the only person you planned a future with isn't here anymore. He's gone. What do you do with a change like that? How do you go by it?

The day of the funeral had now arrived, and I knew that it was going to be brutal. I didn't know how I was going to get through it. I prayed in the morning and asked God to give me courage. Sedrick's brothers and sisters, nieces, and nephews were gathering at the house and getting dressed for the funeral. I had Sedrick's good suit picked up from the dry cleaners for the funeral director to dress him in. I couldn't believe he had worn that same suit to a friend's wedding just a few months before. Now Sedrick would be buried in it, and the thought was unbearable – each element seemed to carry the weight of his absence, turning what used to be ordinary into a collection of heart-wrenching reminders.

The realization hit me like a ton of bricks: life was now a series of moments punctuated by the void left by Sedrick. It was an unexpected and painful journey through the ordinary, where even the most mundane things triggered waves of grief. The funeral day became more than just a goodbye; it became a journey through a landscape now irrevocably altered by the echoes of a life that should have continued. I went with my sister-in-law Sheila to take his suit to the funeral home, along with a beautiful love letter that I had written to him. I wrote everything that I felt about him and asked the funeral director if she could put the letter in his pocket. Sheila asked her to be gentle with him when she dressed him, and I heard the sadness in her voice. After I got dressed, one of Sedrick's nephews drove me to the Church of God on Great Georges Street. I had to be there early to greet the hearse. I felt very shaky as I watched it pull up to the church and Sedrick's casket carried in. The funeral home director stood there, opening the casket, and once again, she asked me to confirm that this was indeed my husband. As I looked inside, seeing Sedrick dressed in that suit, tears welled up, and I nodded, acknowledging that it was him. The reality of the moment hit hard – my husband, lifeless, lying there in front of me. It was a surreal and agonizing truth, like he was right there but also impossibly distant.

As mourners started filling the church, I found myself handing out funeral programs. Putting on a brave face, I tried to smile, express gratitude, and thank everyone for coming. Yet, inside, it felt like a part of me was slowly withering away. Sedrick, my life, was there, right in front of me, and yet, it seemed like he was the farthest from me that one could ever be. The act of thanking people for their presence became a silent plea for someone to bring him back, to undo the inexplicable tragedy that had befallen us. The funeral service was touching, and the pastor delivered a powerful and moving sermon. People in Jamaica are very religious, and funerals are always emotional. "Amazing Grace" and "How Great Thou Art," two of Sedrick's favorite hymns, were sung by the beautiful choir, which almost ripped my heart out. A few family members read tributes and shared loving remembrances, and his Uncle John gave the eulogy. Several times, I kept looking over at Sedrick lying in the casket. I was glad not to have to get up and read my tribute in front of everyone; I really would not have had the strength to do it. I was very thankful that John read it on my behalf.

Finally, the lid was closed for the duration of the service. His nephew Timothy was seated beside me and kept his arm around me for the whole duration of the funeral to help support me. At times, I felt like I might pass out, so I was glad that I had him sitting beside me. I had chosen the song "Gone Too Soon" by Michael Jackson to be played as we were all coming out of the church and the pallbearers were loading the casket back into the hearse. Sedrick loved this song and used to play it all the time, so I thought it would be appropriate for his funeral. After the church service, we all gathered at the graveside to say our final goodbyes to Sedrick. When they started lowering his casket into the grave, everything started spinning, and I felt like I was about to pass out. Seeing his casket going down into the ground hit me hard – it felt so final, like a punch in the gut.

As I stood there, watching them bury him, the thought of living without him seemed impossible. It was like facing this big, scary unknown, and I didn't know if I had what it takes to get through it. Seeing his casket disappear into the ground was like a picture of the huge gap he left in my life.

In that tough moment, the idea of jumping into the grave with him crossed my mind. The pain of him being gone was just too much, and the grave seemed like a way to escape it. It felt like this deep, dark hole that wanted to swallow me up.

The air was heavy with sadness, and as they kept filling up the grave with dirt, it hit me even harder that he was really gone. The graveside became a symbol of the tough road ahead, where every step felt like stumbling through a world that would never be the same without him.

The gravediggers placed a large wooden plank over the grave and began pouring concrete over the top of the cement tomb to seal the grave, as is customary in Jamaica. The preacher started reciting Psalm 23, "The Lord Is My Shepherd," and we all started singing beautiful but sad hymns. I could only imagine what it was like for his brothers and nephew to have to be the pallbearers. When I looked around at all of his relatives who were there, I could see the despair in all of them. None of them could believe that someone had murdered their beloved Sedrick. To think that the only reason he was dead was because, as they say in Jamaica, someone with a "bad" mind had decided to put a bullet in him was unfathomable. They had decided he did not deserve to live and enjoy all he had worked so hard for.

I made a silent promise to him that I would find his killers and have them brought to justice. The agony that I felt in my heart was excruciating, and it truly felt broken. Somehow, I managed to get through the funeral and the burial, and I was relieved that it was finally over. After the funeral, there was a reception at the church with food and refreshments, but I didn't feel like eating anything. I mingled for a little while with all the guests who had come back for the reception. The day was very draining, and I just wanted to go home. Several of my neighbors from Rio Nuevo came to the funeral in a rented bus, and I asked if I could go home with them. I packed my bag at the house and said farewell to Sedrick's family. All of them were very emotional, and this had been a difficult day for all of us. His parents were both deceased. I thought that it was just as well that they were not alive to see that one of their children had been a murder victim. They would have taken it very hard, especially his dear mother. She was a deeply devout woman who loved her son Sedrick very much. The bus trip home took about three hours from there. Yvonne, one of my neighbors who attended the funeral, was concerned for my safety because I was going back to an empty house. She asked me if I would like to go and stay with her in her home for a while. I took her up on her offer and spent a couple of days with her, and I was so relieved that I didn't have to be alone during this time. There are still many good people in the world, and I will never forget the kindness this wonderful lady had shown to me by giving me safe refuge with her temporarily in her lovely home.

Chapter 9
First Christmas Without My Beloved

The first is the worst, it takes you back to day one.

I didn't want to be alone for Christmas in Jamaica, so I decided to fly back to Ottawa to be with Dad. It was my first time flying solo, and it felt kinda strange. The plane was packed with all these cheerful tourists, mostly couples coming back to Canada after enjoying their time in Jamaica. Looking around, it hit me that I was the only one flying solo. It brought back memories of travelling with Sedrick on our trips to Jamaica, and man, I missed him even more.

As the plane cruised through the sky, the happy chatter around me just made the loneliness sink in deeper. It was tough seeing all these couples, knowing that I used to be one of them. The empty seat beside me echoed with the absence of Sedrick, and I couldn't shake off the feeling of being the odd one out.

The flight, which used to be a fun part of our adventures, became a bittersweet journey down memory lane. The familiar scenes outside the window were now a backdrop to the ache in my heart. I wished Sedrick was there with me, sharing those moments, cracking jokes, and making the flight feel less lonely. Instead, it was just me, surrounded by couples and the ghost of memories that seemed to tug at my heartstrings even more. He used to start conversations with people on the plane to find out where they were from and how much they enjoyed their vacations. I have always been nervous when the airplane is taxiing on the runway before taking off, and he used to hold my hand to comfort me. There was no more hand to hold on to, so

I grabbed the armrests and shut my eyes until the plane was in the air. It was all I could do not to burst into tears during the flight, so I focused on watching the onboard movie and doing some word puzzles I had brought along. Travelling would never be the same for me ever again. I arrived at my dad's condo a couple of days before Christmas, and I knew it would be the worst Christmas of my whole life, but I decided I would try my best to get through it.

I was very thankful that I would be with Dad. He was also still feeling very traumatized by the recent events, and we talked about what happened to Sedrick. I knew he was so worried about me, and he was happy that I could come and stay with him. Lily had invited us both to her house for a lovely Christmas dinner with her husband and family. After returning to the condo, Dad and I did some word puzzles and then spent a quiet evening talking. Then I went to my bedroom to get ready for bed, and I spent the rest of Christmas Eve bawling my eyes out, just pining away for Sedrick.

I thought back to all the special Christmases we had together and how much he used to love all the festivities. We used to look forward to putting up the Christmas tree together, and he always helped me with the lights and decorations. We loved giving each other beautiful Christmas presents. It was always our favorite time of the year. Dad and I received an invitation to dinner on Boxing Day from one of his third wife Nadina's grandsons, Miles. He came to pick us up and drove us to his home. It was a family gathering, and along with his wife Brandy and their children, his brother Jay, his wife Jenny, and their three children were there. Everyone was very sympathetic about what had happened, and they all did their best to try and make the day as bright and festive as possible for Dad and me.

Life Interrupted

The rest of the week went by fairly quickly, and while I was in town, I went to have Sedrick's passport cancelled and filled out various forms at our banks and Service Canada to settle his estate. These were all hard tasks for me, but I knew I had no choice but to get them done. One day, Lilly and I went to the grocery store next to the condominium to buy some food for Dad. Unexpectedly, I bumped into Sedrick's friend Richard, who's also Jamaican, and instantly, his face lit up, expecting to see Sedrick with me. When he asked where Sedrick was, I glanced at Lily, feeling a bit lost on what to say. All of a sudden, the terrible story just spilled out of me. I could see the shock on Richard's face, and I knew it hit him hard. His knees buckled, and he swayed like he couldn't comprehend what I'd just told him about his friend. It was tough seeing someone else grapple with the disbelief and pain.

As I shared the heartbreaking news, the weight of the loss not only settled on me but also on Sedrick's friends. Richard's expression went from joyous anticipation to heart-wrenching disbelief in an instant. It hit me that Sedrick wasn't just my husband; he was a friend, a confidant, a part of a community that was now grieving too. The pain wasn't mine alone; it was shared among those who had laughed, celebrated, and created memories with him. The bond they shared was now punctuated with the deep ache of loss, and I realized that, in a way, we were all navigating this unexpected journey of grief together.

We talked a bit longer, and he recalled some of the good times he had shared with Sedrick in Ottawa. Then he gave me his telephone number and told me to call him sometime.

However, I was so exhausted after telling him the story that I wanted to return to the apartment. I didn't even call or see any friends on this trip. All I wanted to do was to stay close to my dad. Everything was still so fresh and raw, and I was so traumatized that I couldn't bring myself to tell any of them what had happened yet. After Christmas was over, it was time to return to Jamaica. I didn't know it then, but I was about to face another raging storm in the coming months…

Chapter 10
Facing Sudden Widowhood

Grief hits you like you're losing the one you love, every day, all over again.

    The first thing I did after I returned from visiting my dad was to have cameras and an alarm system installed in the house and yard to try and make my surroundings safer. There was no way I would stay alone in that house without getting a security system, and that was my number one priority. I also had a sliding bolt door lock installed on my bedroom door to help reinforce the door. It was to help me feel a bit more secure at night when I was in bed.

    The empty lot next door was very bushy, and I paid someone to come and cut down a lot of the thick underbrush to make it harder for anyone to hide there and watch the house. Doing business in Jamaica tests your patience, and processing paperwork takes longer. Things always seem to move slower on an island. The Toyota minibus that we owned had been parked at the family home in Savanna-la-Mar since Sedrick died. He did not have a will, so I discovered it could not be transferred automatically to my name. To sell the vehicle, I would have to go through a lawyer to have a Grant of Administration issued by the Supreme Court in Kingston, which would take almost ten months. Sedrick and I never wanted to talk about death. It was just one of those topics we steered clear of, and we never got around to making any plans in case something happened to one of us. We thought we had tons of time ahead, you know? So, when it hit, we were totally unprepared. The road ahead seemed crazy tough, and I found myself flipping through our old photo albums, getting lost in the memories of our life together.

Tears became a regular thing for me, like a daily ritual. It was hard, but I figured it was better to let it out than keep everything bottled up. Going through those pictures, I could almost feel Sedrick's presence, and at the same time, the emptiness of his absence. It was like reliving the best moments and realizing they were now memories. The future we thought we had was gone, and the present was a constant struggle. Every photo was a bittersweet reminder of the life we had, and I couldn't help but wonder how I was going to navigate this long, uncertain road without him. The tears might've been a daily thing, but in a weird way, they felt like a connection to the pain and love we shared. It was tough, but I guess that's just how grief works – messy, unpredictable, and something you can't neatly put into words. That's when I reread my brochure on grief, and it seemed that I was now somewhere between the third and fourth stages of grieving. The third stage was, for me, a long period of depression, reflection, and loneliness. I realized the full magnitude of my loss, which made me feel empty and full of despair. It was supposed to be just a normal part of the process, and I read that encouragement from others would not be helpful during this time, even though they meant well. Feelings of anger washed over me also, and I blamed those evil monsters for what they had done to my life.

It was the fourth stage of grief, but I tried to control these feelings because I didn't want to be overcome by these strong emotions. Being angry could be detrimental to my health and make my situation worse. So many plans we had made for our life in Jamaica would never come true. Once we could afford it, we had planned on having a beautiful, above-ground pool with a deck built at the back of our property. We were going to complete the steps down to the sea that we had started so that we could put a small boat in the water. Before moving from Canada, Sedrick had bought a small inflatable boat that could seat five or six people. We would have had so much fun taking the boat for little trips along the coastline. Sedrick and I loved to play ping-pong. We would also buy a ping-pong table to put in the yard. I used to look forward to having meals with Sedrick, and it used to be so much fun to prepare our food together. One of the things that hit me the hardest was seeing Sedrick's empty chair at the dining table. It felt like a punch in the gut every time, so I decided to switch things up and started having all my meals at the kitchen island. It was weird, but at least I didn't have that constant reminder right in front of me.

From there, I could gaze out the window at the sea, watching the cruise ships roll into Ocho Rios in the morning and sail away later in the day. It became a routine – a way to distract myself and find some kind of solace in the view. Some days, I didn't really feel like eating much, but I tried to keep it healthy. The struggle was real when it came to cooking for just one person and not wasting food.

Making meals felt different now. It wasn't just about satisfying hunger; it was a solo act in a kitchen that used to be filled with laughter and shared moments. The silence hung heavy, and even the simplest recipes seemed to carry the weight of his absence. Eating alone, staring at that sea view, became a mix of finding comfort in routine and grappling with the loneliness that lingered in every bite. However, I would cook something at least once a week that could last for two or three meals. I also took a daily vitamin and drank a lot of meal replacement drinks such as Ensure because I was determined to keep my energy up and not get too run down. I did everything I could to keep on going.

    Eventually, I bought a laptop computer to replace the stolen one and started doing part-time freelance transcription work. The work involved uploading and listening to online audio files and converting recorded or live human speech into typewritten text. I had to concentrate, and it helped me focus on something other than the murder for a little while. It was also a way to pass the time. Keeping in touch with my friends through emails felt like a vital lifeline. Listening to music and dancing around my living room helped keep me sane and was a great way to relieve some of my stress, and I would sing along to Journey's "Don't Stop Believing' "at the top of my lungs. The song is uplifting and inspirational and has always been a favorite of mine. To keep my morale up, I would watch TV shows that were funny or entertaining. It was too hard to watch violent shows, movies, or the news in the months following the murder. I would read the headlines online to keep up with world events. Finally, I started listening to the news on the radio again. It would still bring back a lot of painful memories whenever I heard about the murders of more innocent people…

Chapter 11
Dad's Grim Diagnosis

What would you do if the one who loved you a lot, starts to forget who you are?

Dad made it a point to call me every single day, sometimes even twice. His voice on the other end always sounded happy, but deep down, I knew he worried about me. Each day, without fail, he'd ask when I was planning to come back and visit. I assured him I'd be there in the spring, not realizing that more tough news was headed my way.

Then, in April 2014, I got a call from him that shook me up. He sounded upset and shared that he had seen a new doctor who gave him something called the Montreal Cognitive Assessment (MoCA). The test didn't go well, and the doctor said something that hit him hard – that he was going to lose his mind one day. Dad got really angry, and I tried my best to calm him down, but he was just distraught. The weight of his distress hit me like a ton of bricks, and I found myself in tears after we hung up. It was tough seeing my dad, who had always been a pillar of strength, facing something so uncertain and scary.

That evening, I called Lily because she was with Dad when the doctor gave him the news. She told me that the doctor said he was starting to develop dementia and that it was just a matter of time before it would begin to get worse. No wonder he was so upset. It must be so frightening to be told this type of news by a doctor. He still had a sharp memory when he came to Jamaica for the last time. He could remember very vivid details about his early childhood and his life. He had just written a beautifully illustrated book about his life story and gave a copy to us on his last visit. He had been in the Army and World War II and had worked many years as a graphic artist. The pain and trauma Dad went through after Sedrick's murder took a toll on his health, and it seemed like it might have played a role in him developing this disease. Trying to understand more, I went online and stumbled upon research funded by the Alzheimer Society. They dug into the connection between PTSD and dementia, and what I found out hit me hard – people with PTSD are twice as likely to develop dementia. It is important to note that having PTSD does not necessarily mean you will definitely develop dementia.

Reading that, it was like a punch in the gut. The worry about how long Dad would have to deal with this weighed heavy on my heart. The idea of him going through such a tough time after everything with Sedrick was just too much. I made up my mind right then – I needed to go back and be with him for a couple of weeks in the spring. It was a mix of sadness, concern, and a determination to be there for Dad, to face whatever was coming together. The uncertainty about the future was tough, but the decision to be there for him felt like a small way to make a big difference.

Chapter 12
Rapid Decline

Grief is a silent storm that rages within, a daily battle between holding on and letting go.

When I stayed with Dad for those two weeks in May, things seemed pretty normal. We spent our evenings tackling word puzzles, and when he talked, he was still sharp and clear. We even hit up a few restaurants and made trips to the mall with Lily. But there was this subtle change.

One day, he got a reminder letter from the Condominium Corporation about those monthly fees. Dad had forgotten to send in the post-dated cheques, and it bothered him more than usual. I tried to calm him down, telling him it happens to everyone, but I could see the frustration on his face. When he sat down to write those twelve cheques, something was off. This simple task that he'd done countless times before became a struggle, and he got visibly upset. It was weird because he'd never had any trouble with this routine stuff during all the years he'd been in the condominium.

During our chats on his balcony, overlooking the swimming pool, I asked him if he wanted to go for a swim. That's when he mentioned a sore on his leg and said he couldn't join in. The mix of frustration, confusion, and this realization that things weren't quite the same was tough to witness. It was like watching a subtle shift, a glimpse into something changing that we couldn't quite put our fingers on. The worry and concern for him started to creep in, and the normalcy we'd had before felt a bit fragile.

He slipped and fell in his bathtub in February and injured his leg badly. When Lily let herself in that day to clean his apartment, she saw a pool of blood all over the floor. She got scared and found my dad in the bathroom bleeding, and she brought him to the Ottawa Hospital Civic Campus Emergency Room. Due to being a Type 2 diabetic, a couple of the open sores had not yet closed up after several months. He had a nurse come every day to dress the leg, and she put a waterproof bandage on it so that he could swim if he wanted to. Swimming was always a favorite activity of my dad, and it kept him in shape. He used to go swimming with his friend Jean, who used to live in the building, every morning, rain or shine. Dad was always a great swimmer and had taught me how to swim at a very early age. Now, it appeared that he had lost his love of swimming. One of the symptoms of developing dementia is losing interest in things you used to love to do. I felt sad that he didn't want to swim anymore. His friend Jean and her husband Ken had moved away from Ottawa but were in town visiting their family. They called us, and we all got together with Lily for dinner one evening at one of my dad's favorite seafood restaurants, Red Lobster. Dad was thrilled to see his friends again and still able to engage in a good conversation with them. We all took a few pictures together on the balcony after dinner, and it was an enjoyable evening. A couple of times during my visit, I had coffee and dinner with some friends I used to work with in my last job, and it was a nice distraction. Having supportive people around me during all of this was a real comfort. Finally, the day to head back to Jamaica arrived, and Dad came down with me in the early morning to see me off in the taxi. As we hugged and said our goodbyes, I promised him that I'd be back soon to visit. Little did I know that the next time I'd see him, things would be a lot different.

Between May and September, I noticed a big change in Dad. He'd sometimes call me in the morning and then ring back about thirty minutes later, not even remembering he'd called before. He'd ask about the day of the week and then forget a couple of minutes later, repeating the same question. These were all signs of dementia, but it was still tough to wrap my head around. The worry for him became constant, and it felt like a never-ending battle with the unknown. The promise to come back and visit weighed heavier on my heart as I grappled with the reality of his changing condition.

I had been reading a lot about the disease on the internet, trying to educate myself as much as possible so I would know what to expect. For anyone who is either a family member or a caretaker who is looking after someone with dementia, The Alzheimer Society website has excellent information on this disease. You can also go to the local library, where they have many good books on the subject, which can help prepare you somewhat for what will happen to your loved one. My next visit to see Dad was in September. Lily had phoned me before I arrived to say that she wouldn't tell him until the day before that I was coming. He was having more and more difficulty remembering important things, like appointments or even taking his medications. When I arrived at his condo early one morning, he was excited that I was there. At first, he made perfect sense while talking to me. However, it didn't take long to see that something was wrong now. The changes I saw firsthand in him were alarming to me. While staying with him this time, he would lock himself in the bathroom and spend over an hour or sometimes longer there. I would worry if he was all right and stand at the door to listen. I could hear him praying, repeating the same prayer over and over. To make him come out, I would knock on the door and tell him I needed to use the washroom. He would start rocking himself while sitting at the dining room table. Then, he would repeatedly grab a tissue from the tissue box, wipe his hands, and throw it in the trash can beside the table. I noticed he didn't make direct eye contact with me anymore, and I had to ask him to look at me constantly to get his attention.

He was having more and more difficulty communicating and engaging in any conversation. Dad kept his art desk and all of his art supplies in the guest bedroom of his condo. Art was always his passion. My dad loved to draw figures and cartoons to keep his hand in every day. He was so good at doing artwork all his life, but now, he didn't even want to draw anymore. Loss of interest in hobbies is just another one of the many symptoms that come with this devastating disease. Eating was becoming another big problem. Dad had little appetite for quite a few years, but now, he barely wanted to eat anything. Lily came and prepared meals for him and stayed for a while to ensure he would eat some food. Otherwise, if she didn't stay with him, he would sometimes go all day without eating. I tried to make him eat while I was there, but it was almost impossible. The rapid weight loss was very frightening to see. Unable to care for his basic needs, he needed help getting dressed. My once dignified father, who had always been such a well-groomed, proud man, was becoming more and more like an infant again. One morning, he was confused. We were supposed to get ready because Lily was coming to pick us up to take him to a medical appointment. After spending almost two hours in the bathroom, he came out still in his pajamas. I told him to get dressed and reminded him about his appointment.

He said he thought it was nighttime and was going back to bed. After Lily arrived, we had difficulty getting him going, and he was crabby. Irritability is another symptom associated with dementia, and it was so hard to see him like this. He used to have such a great sense of humor. We had to be patient with him because it was not his fault. I could see him slipping away from me bit by bit, and it was breaking my heart. While I was there, he sometimes forgot to unplug the portable electric heaters he used to keep warm, which could have been very dangerous. As well as starting a fire in his apartment, he could have put other residents at risk. It was another big safety concern.

One of my step-sisters, Georgia, came over one day after I phoned her. I told her that Lily and I were worried that Dad could no longer live alone and that we needed to have a serious discussion. After we all sat down together, we gently told him he could no longer stay in his condo. For his safety, as well as the safety of others, he would need to go into a retirement home. He got understandably very upset about this and refused. Stubbornly, he said he could manage all alone and did not need to go into a home. I could only imagine how much it must hurt when you have lived independently for so long, and now you're being told you have to go to assisted living. I tried hard not to cry in front of him. None of us were happy about it, but there was no other choice. It would have been selfish of us not to do what was in his best interest. After much coaxing, he finally agreed. Georgia knew of a few long-term nursing homes due to her work as a chair yoga instructor for seniors. She started making some phone calls to see where he could live. That afternoon, we brought him to visit one of the homes, and the director gave us all the information and monthly costs. I had to get up early in the morning to go to the airport to catch my return flight to Jamaica. The last time I left, Dad completely forgot that I was heading out. It was tough waking him up gently, hugging him, saying goodbye, and explaining that I had to go.

This time felt different, and it hit me hard because I knew it might be the last time I'd see him in his condo. Memories of all those visits rushed through my mind, and I could see how content he was living there.

Finding a new place for him took way longer than expected. With the aging population in Ottawa booming, the waitlist for suitable spots was crazy long. Georgia, his caregiver, had her hands full trying to secure a place. It was a frustrating process, but with the help of A Place for Mom, a resource for finding long-term care and retirement homes, things started falling into place. After a ton of calls and persistence, Dad finally moved to the Landmark Retirement Residence in early October.

Leaving him behind in a new place, adjusting to these changes, was a rollercoaster of emotions. The relief of him having a spot mixed with the sadness of leaving his old home behind. It felt like a chapter closing, and I couldn't help but worry about how he'd handle this transition. The uncertainty of it all made the goodbye even harder, and it was like saying farewell to a part of our shared history.

Life Interrupted

I know he was unhappy about it, but he didn't complain too much and tried his best to settle in. Just a few weeks later, I got a call from Lily saying that Dad had developed pneumonia. He had to be taken by ambulance to the hospital and put on oxygen. I called the hospital every day to check on his condition. The nurses told me that he had become weak after being in bed for so long, and they were trying to get him mobile enough to go back to the retirement home. He had also developed some bedsores on his back, which I knew was never a good thing. This time, once he went home, he hardly wanted to get out of bed, which would only weaken him further. The director of the home informed my step-sister one day that they could no longer care for Dad because they didn't have the facilities for dementia patients. The ideal spot for Dad would have been The Perley and Rideau Veterans' Health Centre, a place specifically designed for war veterans in need of long-term care. But, suddenly, things went south, and it felt like we hit a rough patch.

The thought of this facility, tailored to cater to his needs, brought some relief. Yet, the unexpected turn in our plans stirred up a mix of emotions. It was like having a door close just when we thought we had found the right place. Frustration, disappointment, and a sense of urgency crept in as we grappled with the sudden twist in our journey to find the best care for Dad. The uncertainty of what lay ahead added an extra layer of stress, leaving us navigating uncharted territory once again.

Chapter 13
Dad Loses His Battle with Dementia

Losing a loved one is like watching a beautiful sunset; it fades, but the colors linger in our hearts forever.

One night, Dad took a fall and ended up hurting himself, sending him back to the hospital. Lily called me urgently, stressing that I should come see him as soon as possible. The doctor attending to him dropped a bombshell – he was back on oxygen and now dealing with congestive heart failure.

Feeling like I was in a fog, I mustered the strength to call the physician and ask the hard question about how long he had left. The reply hit me like a ton of bricks – he probably wouldn't make it to New Year's. In a daze, I booked a last-minute flight to Ottawa. The reality sunk in slowly, and I couldn't believe I was on the verge of facing another devastating loss, someone I cherished so deeply.

The mixture of shock, sadness, and the looming grief made every step leading up to that flight feel surreal. It was like a whirlwind of emotions, and the weight of the impending farewell hung heavy on my heart. The thought of losing another important man in my life, someone I loved dearly, felt almost too much to bear.

During the flight, I couldn't stop thinking about Dad and Sedrick and almost burst into tears several times. I managed to fight back the tears because I didn't want people on the plane to wonder what was wrong with me. As if that was not bad enough, the heavy winter snowstorm in Toronto that night forced the cancellation of my connecting flight from Pearson International Airport to Ottawa. I tried to call several different hotels near the airport to see if I could get a room, but they were all full. There were many other flight cancellations, and the hotels were all booked. In that late-night rush to get to Ottawa, I thought about reaching out to some of Sedrick's family in Mississauga, but it felt too late, and I didn't want to bother them. Exhausted and frustrated, the reality hit me – I'd be spending the night in the airport. I found a bench in the terminal, trying to rest my head. But, to make things worse, there was noisy construction going on inside the airport that night. Needless to say, sleep was a luxury I couldn't afford, and by morning, I felt completely drained.

As I boarded the rescheduled connecting flight, a mix of relief and weariness settled in. The night had been rough, but the journey had to go on. The fact that the flight took off without a hitch brought a sense of calm, and I finally touched down safely in Ottawa. The whole ordeal left me feeling physically and emotionally drained, like I'd been through the wringer, and I knew I had to brace myself for the challenges that lay ahead.

Once I arrived at the hotel and checked into my room, I caught a bus and went to the General Hospital. I wanted to spend as much precious time as possible with Dad. When I arrived at the hospital and went to his room, I was shocked at how small he looked lying in the bed. He had lost a lot of weight, was very frail, and was so pale. I spent my time holding his hand and talking to him, and he was confused about everything. He wanted to know where he was and what he was doing there. He thought he was back in World War II and was in an army hospital. Lily was also there and tried to get him to eat something after the nurse brought him his lunch. He barely touched anything and seemed only to want to drink liquids. I spent the next few days visiting him at the hospital, and by the third day, when I walked into his room, he stunned me. He stared at me blankly and asked me who I was. I choked back tears, held his hand, and told him I was his daughter Donna. Then he replied, "But this is the first time I'm seeing you," and asked me where I was from. It is the saddest feeling to know that your parents can no longer recognize you. Afterward, I asked the nurse if I could speak to the attending physician to find out how he was doing. The doctor's words were grim, and it hit me hard when they said there wasn't much more they could do for Dad. That day in the hospital, as we sat together, he suddenly looked up, pointed, and called out, "Dad, you're here." It sent shivers down my spine because I had read that near the end of their life, dementia patients often see deceased loved ones. It was both eerie and frightening.

After leaving the hospital, I rushed back to my lonely hotel room and just broke down in tears. All I wanted was Sedrick to be there with me. His comforting presence would've meant the world to me during this tough time, and the longing for him grew even stronger. A couple of days later, Georgia got a call from The Perley and Rideau Veterans' Health Centre, letting her know they had a room ready for Dad. It was a tiny bit of good news in the midst of all the hardship, knowing he would get better care there.

A part of me held out a bit of hope that once there, maybe Dad would rally back a little. He was transferred there by ambulance, and I headed there the next day. Georgia was already there with him when I arrived. The nurse on duty came in and met with us to explain how they would care for him. They even had a lift there to try and get him out of bed and sit him up in a special wheelchair. She explained that they would put a lot of thick mats all around the bed because they do not use railings on their beds. If my dad were to fall out of bed, the mats were there to give him some padding on the floor. At that point, the attending physician came into the room and introduced herself to us. I asked her about Dad's condition in the hallway, and she did not sugarcoat it. She told us that he was a very, very frail and sick man, but they would try their best to make him comfortable. He now only weighed about 95 pounds or less.

A nurse brought in a meal tray for him, but this time, he didn't even want to eat anything. All he wanted were a few sips of water. They had to thicken Dad's water to prevent choking, and on his tray, there was a bowl of glycerin sticks. The nurse explained that we should moisten his lips and tongue with them now and then. It's a tough reality that when dementia patients reach the end of their lives, even swallowing becomes a challenge. I knew from my readings that when they stop eating, it's not starvation but a sign that their organs are shutting down, and they don't need food anymore. Still, watching someone you love go through this is devastating.

Georgia eventually left, and I stayed with Dad, just holding his hand. He began asking me questions about his old workplace, but suddenly, he looked worried. It felt like time was slipping away, and the weight of the situation hung heavy in the room. The mix of helplessness and the imminent loss of someone so dear was almost too much to bear.

He asked me whether he had ever made any money at all. That little part of his memory was now gone. I reminded him that he used to have a great career as a very talented graphic artist. Even though he no longer knew who I was, he asked me if I was doing all right, and I told him that I was doing just fine. Bravely, I tried very hard to keep smiling at him and told him not to worry about me. I stayed with him for as long as I could that day until it was time to leave. Dementia is a cruel, debilitating disease that even robs the person of proper speech patterns.

Talk to your loved one, even when they can no longer communicate well. They also respond well to touch, so holding or massaging their hands is a great way to keep that connection. Every time I visited Dad, he seemed to enjoy holding my hand. Sitting there and still feeling the warmth of his hand was a precious gift to me, and I treasured every moment I had left with him. The next day, I bought him a Christmas card and some nice, cozy flannel pajamas to keep him warm before seeing him. All Dad had to wear was this tiny cotton gown with ties in the back, and I worried he might be too cold. When I got to The Perley, I mentioned the pajamas I bought for him to the nurse, but she said he couldn't wear them. She didn't explain why, so I hurried to his room. Overnight, things had taken a scary turn. Dad was tossing and turning in bed, yanking off his oxygen mask and trying to get rid of his gown. He didn't even register my presence, and it freaked me out. I called the nurse, and she rushed in.

Life Interrupted

She explained that Dad had fallen out of bed again, tearing his skin in a few spots that had gotten really thin. But the worst part was the news that he was slipping into a coma and on the verge of passing away. She mentioned that dementia patients often get really restless just before losing consciousness. I couldn't hold back the tears, and the nurse pulled me into her arms for comfort. I ended up pouring my heart out, sharing the trauma of what Dad had witnessed, thinking it might have played a part in his dementia. The mix of sadness, fear, and the helplessness of watching someone you love fade away was overwhelming.

She agreed with me that it would have been a factor. Another nurse came in, and they were both trying to console me, and they told me that all of this was too much for one person to bear. I didn't want to be alone in the room with him if he should pass away, so I asked one of the nurses to call Georgia and Lily. While I waited for them to arrive, I kept kissing him on the forehead, stroking his hair, and telling him repeatedly that I loved him. In a gentle voice, I told him it was okay if he wanted to go and rest and that I would understand. I was trying to let him know it was all right to let go, even though it was killing me inside. His body, worn and battered, was finally surrendering, and I could sense that he was ready to let go. It was a tough reality to accept, knowing there was nothing more anyone could do. I braced myself for what was coming. When Lily and Georgia arrived a bit later, I asked the nurse if she could arrange for a pastor or clergyman to give Dad last rites. A compassionate Catholic priest joined us, offering prayers and anointing Dad's head with oil.

The only sign of response I got from Dad was when he suddenly grabbed both my hands and held on tight while the priest performed the last rites. I couldn't tell if it was just a reflex or if, in some small way, he understood what was happening. His hands felt as cold as ice, and the mix of emotions – from the solemnity of the moment to the heartache of watching someone you love slip away – was indescribable. The realization that this was the final goodbye was heavy on my heart, and I clung to the small gestures that felt like a connection, even in the face of such profound loss.

After he finished giving my dad last rites, the priest spent a few more minutes consoling Lily and Georgia and I and then left a short time later. The nurse came back in and asked me if my dad liked music. I told her that he loved big band music, and she said she would go and find some music to play for him on the CD player to try and calm him down. Before we left that evening, I turned and looked at him with tears in my eyes. I realized this would be the last time I would see him alive. After returning to my motel, I spent a sleepless night thinking I would get the bad news at any moment. Before going to bed, I called the airline to see if I could get my return flight changed to a later date. Unfortunately, flights to Jamaica were all booked because it was too close to Christmas. I flew back to Jamaica the next day but felt terrible about it. The sad news came by telephone on Sunday, December 21, the day after I arrived home. At least Dad wasn't alone when he passed. Some of Nadina's family members were there at his bedside. When I got the news, the rest of the day was a blur of tears. It felt like my soul was crying, and I couldn't make it stop. In just a little over a year since Sedrick's brutal murder, I had now lost my dad. The grief for Sedrick was still raw, and now I found myself mourning all over again. It felt like the killers had taken another innocent victim.

It was just three days before Christmas, and the thought of celebrating was the last thing on my mind. Losing loved ones makes holidays incredibly painful, and I wondered how I was going to get through it. The weight of sorrow was heavy, and the season's festivities felt like an insurmountable challenge. Coping with the void left by their absence became the new, harsh reality.

I received a telephone call from my neighbor Gwen. She invited me to come and have Christmas dinner with her and her husband, Eddy. I didn't feel like going, but I was very grateful for the invitation, so I forced myself to dress up and spend the afternoon with them on Christmas Day. They had prepared a lovely Christmas dinner. They were returning residents who had been living in England for many years. Ever since Sedrick and I moved to our house, they were always helpful to us. On the day Sedrick passed away, Gwen, a retired nurse, was one of the neighbors who came in to help clean up all the blood. Their kindness is something I'll never forget. Even though Christmas remained a somber time for me, their support made it a bit brighter, and I was grateful not to spend it alone.

In the midst of the sadness, their generosity and care became a silver lining. It was like a small ray of light breaking through the dark clouds, bringing a sense of warmth and connection during a time when loneliness threatened to take over. Their simple acts of kindness became a lifeline, helping me navigate through the holiday season, which had become a constant reminder of the losses I had suffered.

Chapter 14
Preparing for A Second Sad Farewell

Amidst the pain of goodbye, the echoes of love remain...

After Christmas and New Year's, I had to gather the strength to start arranging my dad's funeral. Dad's two stepdaughters, Georgia and Kati, were on board to help with the arrangements, and they put me in charge. It felt like déjà vu, having to plan another funeral after going through it for my husband. Dad had already been cremated, sticking to his wishes, so we decided on a Celebration of Life ceremony instead of the usual funeral service. The three of us began brainstorming ideas, exchanging emails back and forth.

The mix of emotions during this process was overwhelming. It was like diving back into a painful task that I had hoped wouldn't come around again so soon. The effort to celebrate his life while dealing with the fresh grief was a delicate balance. It felt like juggling sorrow and remembrance, and every decision became a reflection of the love and loss we were grappling with.

I started by ordering some beautiful red roses to put beside the urn and another bouquet of red roses and blue orchids to place in a vase on the table. We also decided that we were going to put together a couple of photo collages showcasing Dad's life, and I started to look for some photos to bring with me. I had a lovely photo portrait of him enlarged and framed. After searching the internet, I found a touching poem I wanted to read at the service. I also found a couple of Scriptures in my Bible that I wanted to recite. I also chose a couple of beautiful hymns, which I thought would be very appropriate. I booked my flight and hotel room online for Ottawa on January 26, 2015. The service was planned for January 31, 2015, at the Landmark Retirement Residence, just four days after my birthday. When I arrived in Ottawa, it was cold, and the wind chill made it feel like -30 degrees Celsius, but at least it was bright and sunny. My hotel was right across the street from a major shopping Center, which was handy for me to walk to. The next few days flew by, and I met Lily for lunch on my birthday. I also met with two other friends for dinner and coffee. We had kept in touch by email since Sedrick and I moved to Jamaica. Georgia and Kati had been pillars of moral support after I lost Sedrick, and once again, they were by my side when I lost my dad. Georgia, especially, extended her kindness by inviting me over for dinner on my birthday along with her husband, Alan. The plan was to work on the photo collages and program for the service while I was there. To my surprise, they went the extra mile and prepared a lovely dinner to celebrate my birthday, complete with a red velvet cake for dessert.

The gesture hit me right in the heart. Sedrick always knew how much I loved red velvet cake and made sure to order one for my birthday. Having them recreate that tradition, especially during such a challenging time, was both heartwarming and bittersweet. The mix of sadness for those who were no longer there and the warmth of the love surrounding me was a testament to the strength of friendship and the power of shared memories.

It was a weird coincidence because Georgia and Alan didn't even know that I loved red velvet cake! I thought it was a little sign from Sedrick that he was near me on my birthday. After dinner, we called Father Daryold, the Catholic priest at Lily's church, to ask him for assistance in putting our Order of Service together. We had asked him to officiate the service and give a Catholic homily for Dad. He was more than happy to assist us and gracious in helping us make up the Order of Service. My other step-sister Kati asked us to include a traditional Hawaiian reconciliation ritual called Ho'oponopono in the service. It would be meaningful because Dad loved Hawaii and had visited twelve times while married to his wife, Nadina. Now, we finally had our Order of Service, and I would be able to get the programs printed up in the morning. I felt a sense of relief as the plans for the service started falling into place, assuring me that it would be a beautiful and fitting tribute to Dad. The night before the service, I settled down in my hotel room to write a tribute letter to him. It was my chance to pour out all the love I felt, reflecting on his life and expressing how profoundly grateful I was to be his daughter.

The emotions were intense as I put pen to paper. It was a mix of gratitude for the moments we shared, the love he gave, and the impact he had on my life. But there was also an undeniable sadness, knowing this was my final farewell, my chance to say everything I wished I could have said when he was still with us. The act of writing became a cathartic process, a way to navigate through the complex emotions that come with losing someone so dear.

Chapter 15
Dad's Story

In the dance of sorrow, hope is our steady partner, leading us towards a new dawn.

My dad, born in Kingston, Ontario, on July 9, 1917, had a brother named Bill. Their dad served in the Canadian Army, and after Dad was born, they moved to Côte-St.-Luc, Quebec. They lived there for about six years. When he was eight, his grandfather got sick in England. Dad, along with his mom and brother, visited his grandparents in Hythe, Kent, on the English Channel near Dover, for about a year. After that, the army sent my grandfather to Regina, Saskatchewan. So, it was time for Dad, his mom, and brother to head back to Canada.

Life Interrupted

Reflecting on his early years stirred a mix of feelings. There was a sense of nostalgia and curiosity about the places and moments that shaped his childhood. It was like peering through a window into his past, understanding the twists and turns that led him to where he was. Each memory carried a unique emotion, weaving together a tapestry of experiences that contributed to the man he became.

After living in Regina for a few years, his father retired from the army and decided to move to Vancouver, British Columbia. My dad was now in grade six when they all moved there. He used to tell me how much he loved living in Vancouver. Dad attended the B. C. College of Arts and the Vancouver School of Art and took lessons from F.H. Varley, one of the artists who made up the Group of Seven. He learned figure drawing and commercial art while taking art classes two nights a week. For a while, he did work in commercial art, but it was the Great Depression, and it was hard to find any job or earn any money at that time. During that period, Dad made a significant decision to volunteer for the army, joining the permanent force in 1937 in Esquimalt, near Victoria, B.C. In 1941, amidst World War II, he became part of an elite regiment, B Squadron of the Princess Louise Dragoon Guards. His war journey unfolded from 1941 to 1945, taking him to England and Italy. It was during this time in the army that he started drinking.

As he shared this part of his life with me, there was a mix of pride and sorrow. Pride for the courage it took to step up and serve during such a challenging time, yet sorrow for the toll it took on him. The revelation about soldiers turning to alcohol as a way to cope with the horrors of war brought a deeper understanding of the sacrifices made by those who served. It was a complex tapestry of emotions, acknowledging both the bravery and the scars left behind by that chapter in his life.

One day, he learned that in the twenty months between July 1943 and February 1945, almost six thousand Canadian soldiers had died in Italy! I looked at the medals awarded to him for his service and felt very proud of him for his bravery during one of the darkest periods of our history. Every year, he attended the Remembrance Day Ceremony at the National War Memorial and used to wear his medals proudly displayed on his lapel. After the war ended, and while he was still in the army, he lived in Montreal, Quebec. One day, he saw a job posting in the art department saying they were looking for a graphic artist. Out of the blue, he went in and applied. The man in charge of the art department asked him to hand-letter a sign to demonstrate his art skills and was so impressed by him that he hired him on the spot. Dad had also met my mother, who was working in the army mess hall while he was there. They began dating and got married in 1957. My parents got married later in life. Unfortunately, he had become addicted to alcohol by this time, and this was wreaking havoc on his life. Before I was born, he met a man who took him to an Alcoholics Anonymous Meeting and sponsored him.

Dad joined in 1961. He credited AA with saving his marriage, career, and his life. After I was born in 1962, I never saw him drink one day my entire life. I greatly admire his strength and willpower to quit drinking and regain his life. He had remained sober for over 50 years. What an accomplishment! Mom was 41 years old when I was born, and I was an only child. Dad had taken me to movies when I was small and taught me how to swim and ride a bicycle. He stayed in Montreal until 1968. When it was time to leave the army, Dad applied for a graphic artist position in the Public Service of Canada in Ottawa and got hired. He moved to Ottawa and stayed at the YM/YWCA for a few months, and my mother and I eventually moved from Montreal to join him in Ottawa. When school was out for the summer, I used to love going to his office with him for the day whenever I could. He did cartooning and graphic arts and made a lot of hand-printed signs. I marveled at all the beautiful, colorful artwork he would create at his art desk. I was so glad that he worked at what he loved. Art was his lifelong passion, and it made him very happy. It gave him a great career in the Public Service until he retired in 1981. After retirement, he took me to visit my grandmother in Victoria, BC, for a month-long holiday.

 I was very excited because I hadn't flown on a plane before. Dad and I had a great time on the flight, and he even took me into the cockpit to see how the pilot and co-pilot flew the plane. We stayed with my grandmother and had a wonderful time. My grandmother had lived in Montreal for a few years but had decided to move to an apartment in Victoria when I was still a child. She was living in Esquimalt, and her building was right beside the Pacific Ocean, with a spectacular view. While we were there, Dad took me to the famous Butchart Gardens in Victoria and many other beautiful sights on the island. We took my grandmother to Vancouver for the day and to Chilliwack, and she was so happy. This trip was one of the highlights of my life. My mother passed away on July 18, 1988, from a pulmonary embolism, and Dad, Sedrick, and I were all very shocked and saddened by her sudden death.

It was a very traumatic event for me. Unfortunately, she never liked going to the doctor. It turned out she had a blood clot in her leg, which had travelled to her lungs. She got rushed to the hospital, but it was too late. After she died, Sedrick and I started a weekly tradition of going to Sunday brunch with Dad. We wanted to help keep his spirits up. I knew that he was feeling very lonely. In the summer of 1989, my dad had gotten introduced to a lady named Nadina by her grandson Chad, a lifeguard who worked at the swimming pool at Dad's condominium. On their first date, they had gone for ice cream and seemed to hit it off quickly. They got married in 1990 and enjoyed many years of happiness together until she passed away in 2007 after a brave battle with cancer. Poor Dad took it very hard, and he was heartbroken. Nadina's family remained close to my dad, and he had been a big part of their family. Every day since she died, he would pray the AA Serenity Prayer: "God grant me the serenity to accept the things I cannot change, the courage to change the things I can, And the wisdom to know the difference."

Sedrick and I always spent as much time with him as possible. We even took Dad on a couple of car trips to Montreal, Quebec, and he was thrilled to visit all the places he used to go to when he lived there. He also enjoyed movies, and we used to go to the cinema together or rent movies at our house to watch with him. Despite having vision problems in his left eye and Type 2 diabetes, Dad maintained his independence remarkably well for many years. He didn't face mobility issues, never relying on a walker or a cane. He stayed active, making a routine of swimming every day, reading, and hopping on the bus to visit his favorite shopping malls. Alongside these activities, he cherished time with friends and had a fantastic sense of humor.

Reflecting on his vibrant life brought a mix of emotions. There was a sense of admiration for how he continued to enjoy life, staying engaged in activities he loved. Yet, the awareness of the inevitable longing for him tugged at my heart. Our father-daughter bond was filled with love, and the thought of missing him deeply loomed in the background. The gratitude for the wonderful life he led mingled with the sadness of realizing that our cherished moments together were now memories.

Chapter 16
The Celebration of Life Ceremony

Through the cracks of brokenness, hope sprouts like a resilient flower, reminding us that healing is a journey, not a destination.

After finishing my tribute letter, I felt emotionally drained and headed off to bed, hoping for some much-needed rest before the service the next day. Morning came too quickly, and my emotions were all over the place. I went to the hotel restaurant for breakfast, but eating was a struggle. The nerves were getting to me because I had to read the poem and tribute letter I had chosen for Dad in front of everyone at the service. I wasn't sure how it would go, and the fear of breaking down in front of everyone loomed large. Still, I tried to gather my courage, telling myself I could do it, and said a prayer for strength.

After putting on my black dress and fixing my hair and makeup, it was time to catch a bus and go to the Landmark Retirement Residence. When I arrived, I was the first one there. I went to the room where we would be holding our service. It was a lovely room with a fireplace, and the chairs and tables were all set up. As I unwrapped the flowers that had already arrived, a mix of emotions swirled within me. Soon after, my step-sister Georgia and her husband Alan joined, bringing with them the urn and the photo collages. It was a poignant moment, and my cousin Megan, who had come all the way from Detroit, Michigan, was there too. Dad had a deep connection with his brother Bill, who passed away from cancer before I was born, and Megan is Bill's daughter.

Life Interrupted

The gathering of family and the tangible reminders of Dad's life brought both comfort and sorrow. Seeing the urn and the photos, knowing the significance they held in our shared history, stirred a complex mix of emotions. The presence of loved ones, both near and far, added a layer of support amidst the weight of loss. It was a poignant moment, where memories and connections became a bridge between the past and the present.

We started talking, and I was happy that she was there. When I saw the urn containing Dad's ashes, I felt overcome with sadness. We spent the next half hour or so setting up the room and a display table where I placed Dad's war medals. Everything looked lovely after it was all set up, and now I just needed to get my nerves under control. People who knew my dad in his condominium building and friends and family members from Nadina's family started to arrive. I greeted everyone, handed out the programs, and started getting everyone seated. My friend Cari and her husband Sylvain had also come to the service, and I was happy to see them there to support me in my time of need. Once Father Daryold arrived, it was time to get the service underway. The service turned out to be very beautiful, moving, and very emotional. We selected two hymns, "Amazing Grace" and "Abide with Me." These hymns are played during Remembrance Day Ceremonies and are very meaningful. Father Daryold delivered a touching Catholic homily to my dad. With hands trembling, I read my chosen poem and tribute letter, managing to hold it together until the end of the letter, where I broke down a bit. After reading, I carefully placed the letter beside the urn. Then, several members of Nadina's family and my cousin Megan shared their own heartfelt remembrances. As the service concluded, one of the kids distributed packets of Flanders Poppy seeds to all the guests, and I asked everyone to plant them in the spring as a remembrance for my dad.

The act of sharing memories and the gesture with the poppy seeds brought a mix of emotions. There was vulnerability in expressing my feelings in front of everyone, yet there was also a sense of relief in letting those emotions out. The collective sharing of memories from others underscored the impact Dad had on many lives. The idea of planting poppy seeds added a touch of hope and continuity, turning a somber moment into a symbol of remembrance and new beginnings.

I chose this keepsake because the poppy symbolizes remembrance of war veterans. We played the song by Andre Rieu titled "Time to Say Goodbye" as we all held hands. My dad loved Andre Rieu, so this song was deeply personal. It was a fitting and loving tribute to a man who had led a meaningful life. I grew up with a wonderful, kind, sweet father with such a big heart. Even though I was in deep mourning for Dad and still grieving for Sedrick, I was able to hold up for the service. After the service, I had dinner with Georgia, Alan, and Megan. My cousin Megan and I exchanged email addresses before I left and promised to keep in touch with each other. I knew that I would miss the daily phone calls with my dad. It used to be so wonderful to hear the sound of his voice. He had been so worried about me following Sedrick's murder. Perhaps if the killers had been caught before Dad fell ill, it might have brought him some peace of mind. Now, he'd never know who had caused such pain to our family. The next day, I had a flight back

Life Interrupted

to Jamaica, set for early morning, and I wasn't eager about it. These unexpected, life-altering events shook me to my core. They blindsided me, catching me off guard. It was the first time I felt completely alone in the world and extremely vulnerable. The weight of grief and uncertainty made the journey ahead seem daunting.

Chapter 17
In Survivor Mode

Grief is the price we pay for love, a currency of the heart that makes our memories priceless.

Coming back home, the once familiar silence felt eerily haunting in the now big, empty house. Living in survivor mode, I became hyper-vigilant. Every unexpected noise made me jump, thinking someone might be breaking in again. Eventually, I realized it was just the strong ocean breeze causing doors to slam. One night, a vase broke in the upstairs bathroom, and the sound of shattering glass sent me into a panic. The house, once a place of comfort, had transformed into a space where every creak and crack triggered a heightened sense of vulnerability and fear.

Vivid images and constant flashbacks of the break-in and murder haunted me, and I was having recurring nightmares. Some nights, I dreamt that I could see Sedrick walking in a large crowd, and it looked like he was searching for me. I would call to him, and he would start walking towards me with a smile, and then suddenly, he would disappear back into the crowd again. There are power failures in Jamaica now and again, and there were a couple of nights when all the lights went out while I was sitting down watching television. I got worried, thinking that maybe someone would pick that time to try and break in again since the alarm system and cameras didn't work when the power was gone. The only thing to do was light a few candles in the living room and sit there, hoping the electricity would soon come back on. When all the lights were off in the neighborhood, it looked so dark and scary, especially since I was alone in the house! One night, while in bed, the garage door opened unexpectedly, and the sound sent shivers down my spine. Convinced that someone was coming in, my knees were trembling as I switched on the light and headed downstairs to investigate. To my relief, there was nobody there. The incident heightened the constant fear and unease, turning the haven of my home into a place where even the smallest noises triggered a rush of anxiety and apprehension.

The automatic driveway gate opened another night, which was very odd. After that, I bought a chain with a padlock and put it around the gate so it couldn't open again. I phoned the security company that had installed the gate to report it. The technician told me that these electronic devices sometimes malfunction. On a few occasions, the alarm went off in the middle of the night, which startled me out of bed and sent my heart racing. I'd look at the cameras to see if anyone was there, but I could not see anyone. The alarm systems were so sensitive that even a bat flying around could trigger them. Every night, as I went to bed, I kept a machete underneath the mattress and a knife under my pillow, just in case I needed to defend myself. All I could do was pray, asking God to protect me and help me get through the night. Every little sound put me on edge, and my nerves were constantly on the verge of breaking. The overwhelming sense of vulnerability turned my nightly routine into a ritual of fear and desperate hope for safety.

I was lucky to get two hours of sleep a night, and I always felt a little relief when morning came, knowing that I had made it through another night unharmed. The police patrolled the neighborhood occasionally, stopped by my gate, and warned me several times to be especially cautious. There have been cases where murderers came back a second time when they did not get all of their intended targets. They would sometimes wait a year or more and try again. To think that I still had a price on my head was very frightening. Whenever I went outside to water the garden or play with Sandy, my dog, I always brought a small container of pepper spray tucked into my clothes. It is legal in Jamaica to carry pepper spray with you. I figured that if someone did try anything again, I would not go down without trying to put up a fight. I kept pepper spray handy, thinking if I could spray it in someone's eyes, it might buy me some time to escape. I was cautious in the yard, fearing someone could easily jump over the wall and catch me off guard. I made sure not to linger outside for too long. The upstairs veranda, offering a view of the front yard, became my safe spot, where I could sit and gaze at the garden in the afternoons. I hired a local gentleman to handle the grass-cutting every few weeks, sparing me from doing it myself. The memories of long evening walks around the neighborhood with Sedrick became a bittersweet contrast to the newfound precautions and anxieties in this unfamiliar territory.

Now, it wasn't safe for me to go for a walk anymore. After all, the murderers knew what I looked like and could easily recognize me if they saw me again. Instead, I would run up and down the stairs for twenty to thirty minutes and use my dumbbells for exercise, which gave me a pretty good workout. I had virtually become a prisoner in my own home, and I lost my freedom. It made me feel as though I had been given a life sentence and was living on lockdown in solitary confinement. One day, I was washing something in the laundry room sink and thought I heard a male voice calling my name. It made me stop running the water, and I went to see if someone was at the front gate. One early Sunday morning, I thought I heard someone, but when I looked, there was nobody there. It felt eerie, the silence disrupted by imaginary sounds. Another morning, I caught a glimpse of what seemed like a man running alongside the house from the corner of my eye, yet, once again, there was no one. It left me questioning my own sanity, wondering if the stress and fear were playing tricks on my mind. The constant state of alertness was taking a toll, making me question reality and adding a layer of psychological strain to the already challenging situation.

Occasionally, I received invitations to neighbors' homes for dinner, and I also went into Ocho Rios a couple of days a week to eat lunch downtown. A very kind man named Lester lived in the neighborhood, and he drove me to town and brought me to Kingston when I needed to go and get some paperwork sorted out. I always felt like it was never safe for me to go out alone anywhere. He would drive down to check on me to see if I was all right or needed anything. Whenever he heard a house alarm going off in the neighborhood at night, he would call me to see if it was mine. I had his cellphone number, and he told me to call him, no matter what time it was, in case I had an emergency. Thank goodness I had someone there that I could count on for help when I needed it. I could not believe I was living on this beautiful, tropical, lush island and could no longer enjoy it. It was not the same anymore without Sedrick. He was the whole reason why I came to live in Jamaica in the first place. It hurt when I went outside and looked at all the beautiful flowers and palm trees we had planted together and saw how hard we had worked to make the place look nice. Even looking at the car in the garage was too much for me. He loved that little red Honda Civic, and I could still picture him spending hours washing and taking care of it. I couldn't bring myself to go back to the beach in Ocho Rios, a place we used to love. The thought of swimming, knowing he'd never be there with me again, was just too painful.

We shared so many joyful moments there, having swimming races and ending up breathless from laughter, especially when I usually beat him. The beach, once a source of happiness, now carried the weight of loss. The cruel actions of someone had snatched away those joyful times. Mentally, I felt tormented by the haunting memories of what occurred in that house, as if I were trapped in a tomb. The negative energy in the home added to the overall sense of despair and grief.

Every time I sat down in the living room to watch television, I could still see the exact spot where Sedrick had taken his last breath and could still picture all of that blood. Even though the sofa that he had died on was long gone, the images in my head were crystal clear and ingrained in my memory. I never told anyone, but after the deaths of Sedrick and Dad, I became very depressed, and there was one day that I was feeling despondent. I was outside for a few minutes, sitting on the stone wall at the back of our house when suddenly, I felt like giving up. I started to cry, and tears were running down my cheeks. I wondered if life was worth living now that my two favorite men were both gone. My mind took a dark turn, and I found myself thinking about what it would be like to jump off the wall and vanish beneath the sea waves. Out loud, I wondered, "Who would miss me now?" It was a place I had never been mentally, contemplating something I had always strongly believed against – taking my own life. Then, thoughts of Dad and Sedrick surfaced. I knew how deeply they loved me, and I realized they wouldn't want me to hurt myself. Their memory became a lifeline, a reminder that there were reasons to keep going, even in the midst of the overwhelming pain.

Thankfully, I managed to snap myself out of it., but my demons overcame me momentarily. I made a promise to myself that if I ever had any thoughts about suicide again, I would go and see a doctor immediately. Luckily, those thoughts never crossed my mind again. I just had to keep fighting and putting one foot in front of the other, no matter what. I was now at a crossroads in my life, but after a few more months, I finally decided to put the house up for sale. It was a very emotional decision, but it was something that I knew I had to do. I took steps to prepare the house for sale, getting a guy to paint the outside and the iron fence and gate. Then, I reached out to a Remax Jamaica real estate agent. We went through all the paperwork and listing details. Now, it's a waiting game for someone to make an offer. Some neighbors expressed concern about my safety, wondering why I hadn't moved already. Mostly, it's about the money – moving comes with its own costs, and I have to weigh my options carefully. The process of selling the house became a mix of hope for a new start and financial practicality amid the challenges.

I wanted to use proceeds from the house sale to purchase another home, and I also wanted to make sure that I was around to maintain the house properly until it got sold. After all we had invested in the house, I didn't want to abandon the place. In addition, I had to wait for the paperwork to be completed on the minibus so I could have it transferred to my name and then sell it. Most of all, I wanted to be there in case the police made an arrest soon, and I would have to go and identify the suspects. It wasn't easy to stick around, but I would try and tough it out for as long as possible. I was confused about where I wanted to move if the house got sold and whether to return to Ottawa or move to a different part of Canada to make a fresh start. Another option I considered was to buy a condo and stay in Jamaica. I did not think that would be a wise choice, even though I went and looked at a pretty condo in St. Ann's Bay, which had 24-hour security, a lovely infinity pool, and a grocery store on site. There is something so comforting about having your life partner by your side to share in the decision-making process, and I was having a hard time. I read in a brochure that losing a spouse is one of the most stressful things in life.

Facing the prospect of starting over felt overwhelming, but I had no other option. Despite hating everything that had happened to me, it became clear that this was my new reality. The emotions were a mix of dread, sorrow, and a forced acceptance of a life I never imagined.

Chapter 18
Finding Comfort in Faith

In the dance of sorrow, hope is our steady partner, leading us towards a new dawn.

People say everything happens for a reason, but I couldn't wrap my head around why this happened to us, and maybe I never will. Sedrick, a good, honest man, didn't deserve to die the way he did. Another person's cruelty stole his life, and accepting that fact was a constant struggle. I couldn't fathom how someone could take a life and then act like everything's normal. How do they live with themselves? How do they sleep at night? Turning to spirituality became my refuge. Desperate for answers and a way to cope, I leaned on prayer and immersed myself in the Bible to find strength in the midst of the profound confusion and pain.

On Sunday mornings, I watched a religious program on television called "In Touch With Dr. Charles Stanley." It gave me some comfort to know that God had been with me all along and that He carried me through my darkest hours. As a Christian, I believe that God truly loves each one of us, and He never leaves us, no matter what terrible trials and tribulations we are going through. On the day of the break-in and murder, I felt that He sent his angels there to help Dad, Lily, and me. Maybe the murderers would have killed my dad and Lily for the fun of it, or so they would not leave any witnesses behind. The police would have probably found four dead bodies in the house. If I had stayed downstairs instead of making the snap decision to run upstairs with my phone and call 911, I would have been lying there dead beside Sedrick. I came within inches of losing my life that day when I was hiding in the bathroom, and I didn't think I would survive. God gave human beings free will. I believe Sedrick's murder happened because of jealousy and spite. No one forced his killers to do this; they made that wicked choice. Taking another person's life is never a right anyone has. I trust that God will be the ultimate judge, and they will face the consequences, even if they don't get punished on Earth. I held onto bitterness and anger for a long time, feeling they didn't deserve forgiveness. However, after months of turmoil and prayer, I forgave them. It was for my own peace of mind; I didn't want anger and hatred to harm my health. Even though I forgave, I'll never forget what they did, and I won't support or justify their actions.

Chapter 19
First Anniversary of Sedrick's Death

In the midst of loss, we find strength we never knew we had, and hope that carries us through the darkest nights.

The first anniversary of Sedrick's death slammed into me like a ton of bricks. In Jamaica, it's the family's responsibility to buy a headstone after the burial. On the burial day, the grave is sealed with concrete, and they write the loved one's name on the wet concrete. The weight of this ritual, marking the passage of a year since his passing, brought a flood of emotions. The reality of loss, the absence that became more permanent, hit me hard as I grappled with the solemnity of the occasion.

Sedrick's family and I bought pretty blue tiles to lay on the grave. We also bought a beautifully engraved granite headstone, and everything was ready for November 17, 2014. I made plans to go up to Savanna-la-Mar for the day, and my neighbor Lester picked me up to take me there. Along the way, I purchased lovely red and white roses and some blue helium balloons, as blue was Sedrick's favorite color. Several family members went with me to the grave to mark the occasion. Once everyone arrived at the graveside, we all said a prayer together, and then I tearfully said a few words about Sedrick. Afterward, we released the balloons and watched them soar high up into the sky toward Heaven. We stayed at the graveside, deep in reflection, and later gathered for lunch at a local restaurant. The unfairness of Sedrick being beneath the ground hit me hard, making me feel profoundly sad. He should have been there with us, but instead, his life was abruptly cut short for no good reason. The sadness and frustration overwhelmed me as we marked this solemn occasion.

Coming back on the anniversary had been a brutal reminder that he was in the grave because someone had deliberately put him there. What a terrible price he had paid just for wanting to live in his native country again!

Chapter 20
Leaving Jamaica Behind

The echo of laughter, the shadow of a smile, are like whispers of love, assuring us that the ones we miss are never truly gone.

After a year and seven months, I took a small step toward sorting out my life. My lawyer informed me that the Registrar of the Supreme Court had signed the Grant of Administration letter, allowing me to sell the Toyota minibus. I picked it up the next day, headed to the Tax Office for the vehicle title. The process took months, and getting the Grant felt like a weight lifted. Selling the bus to another JUTA driver was a moment of relief, a potential turning point, giving me a glimmer of much-needed encouragement.

There was one more incident that forced me to decide to leave the island. Somebody had vandalized the For Sale sign that my realtors had installed alongside the main highway. They had chopped down the wooden posts and ripped up the sign in a million pieces in the middle of the night. I had gone out just the day before, and the sign was intact. When I went downtown the next morning, I happened to notice it. At least six other For Sale signs were along the road near mine but were all untouched. Alarmed, I phoned the police to report it, and a female detective drove out to see me. She said that she felt that the killers had done this and saw it as a warning to me. They harbored intense hatred towards me, evident in the malicious destruction of the sign. Maybe they resented that I was still alive and jealous that I would receive money from selling the house. Concerned for my safety, the detective urged me to leave

Jamaica before it was too late. Real estate transactions in Jamaica were sluggish, and in late fall 2015, tired of putting my life on hold and feeling like a prisoner, I decided to rent an apartment in Ottawa, even though the house was still unsold.

I thought it would be the best decision I could make for my safety. I took the policewoman's warning very seriously, and I knew that my life was still in grave danger. Someone may have been planning to come back for me. I couldn't take the chance. Living in that house was no longer an option for me. I knew that if I would have stayed there too much longer, it would have been detrimental to my health, both mentally and physically. I had stayed there by myself for almost two years after the murder, and now it was time for me to go. In the days leading up to my departure from the island, I took a trip back to Savanna-la-Mar to spend a day with Sedrick's family and visit his grave. Saying goodbye to my in-laws was an emotional experience because of the special bond I shared with them. His childhood home held many cherished memories from our vacations together.

Before I knew it, the day had come, and it was time to fly out of Montego Bay. That morning, I walked around the yard one last time, wistfully looking at the beautiful sea view and the lovely garden. I knew this was the right thing to do even though I felt torn up inside. It made me cry to think of all that I had to leave behind after all the hard work and love that had gone into building what was supposed to be our dream home. I was trying very hard to detach myself emotionally and tell myself that it was for the best. My dog Sandy seemed to sense that something was going on, and she was extra excited, jumping around me more than usual. It made me feel sorry for her. My friend Lester agreed to take care of her, giving her a good home.

Life Interrupted

Unfortunately, I couldn't bring her along to the rental apartment because they didn't allow large dogs. I love dogs, so leaving Sandy behind was tough, and I knew I would miss her.

A few months before leaving Jamaica, I had managed to rescue one of the stray kittens that Sedrick and I used to feed in the yard. He was a cute tuxedo cat that I named Mojo, and he would be a great little companion for me. I decided to import him back to Canada, which was quite a lengthy process. There was a lot of paperwork to fill out, several veterinary visits, and making arrangements with Air Canada for his flight. He would be in air cargo on the same flight as me, and I was nervous about his travelling, but he managed well overall. I was happy to see his familiar little face in Canada. Sedrick had loved him very much and used to enjoy playing with him, so I thought it was special to bring him with me. As the plane was taxiing down the runway in Montego Bay, I thought about our hopes and dreams all for naught and how I wished I could have been going home with my beloved Sedrick by my side. It was strange to think that I had come to Jamaica as a happily married woman, and now I was returning to Canada as a lonely widow. The thought made me feel like I was about a hundred years old., although I also felt a sense of relief knowing that I was finally getting out of harm's way.

A strange thing happened during the flight. I sat in an aisle seat and dozed off during the flight while trying to watch a movie. It was an evening flight, and the cabin was dark because the crew had turned off most overhead lights. Suddenly, I awoke with a start because I felt someone tapping me on the shoulder to get my attention. Immediately, I looked around me, but no one was walking in the aisle.

As I looked around, I noticed that everyone around me was fast asleep on the plane. It made me wonder if this was some kind of sign from Sedrick or my dad, as if they were expressing that they were happy to see me leave Jamaica.

Chapter 21
Turning the Page

The pain of parting may linger, but so does the warmth of memories, like a comforting embrace in the cold of sorrow.

When the plane touched down at Pearson Airport in Toronto in the evening, I felt a mix of relief and weariness. I stayed overnight at the Sheraton Airport Hotel and caught my connecting flight to Ottawa the next morning. My friend Cari and her husband Sylvain, being incredibly thoughtful, picked me up from the airport. We spent the day shopping for pet supplies and other household items I needed, and their kindness really touched my heart.

They had even loaned me a folding table and chairs so that I would have a place to eat. I ordered a sofa bed from Sears, and Sylvain helped bring it upstairs to my apartment with a driver I had hired to deliver it. I appreciated all the help and thoughtfulness that my friends gave me. It was a relief to finally be able to go to bed at night without having a knife under my pillow and a machete under the bed, even though I was still hyper-vigilant. Just to be able to go out shopping or to a restaurant without having an escort was so liberating. I had always taken my freedom for granted, and when I had it taken away from me, it did something to my psyche. For the first time since Sedrick and Dad passed away, I decided to put up some decorations and a Christmas tree that December. It was a bit tough, realizing that my two special guys wouldn't be there to celebrate Christmas with me. I tried my best to make the holiday season a bit brighter, finding strength and comfort by focusing on the true meaning of Christmas.

To honour them both at Christmas, I donated some money to the Salvation Army and the World Wildlife Fund, two of their favourite charities, in memory of them. It was important to me to continue to find ways to honour my loved ones to feel like they were still a part of my life. Just a week before Christmas, I went out into the community and got involved with some volunteer work to help collect food donations for needy families. It felt good for my soul to be able to donate some of my time to help a good cause. Since I had a second chance at life, I wanted to give something back. Getting involved in volunteering had always been a fulfilling experience for me, and I was eager to continue it. On Christmas Eve, I attended a Mass, finding solace in the familiar traditions. The evening was spent with Lily and her family, creating a unique bond. We shared the difficult moments of being in the house together on the day Sedrick passed away and navigating through my dad's illness. These shared experiences brought us closer, providing a sense of understanding and support during challenging times.

Those tragic events brought us closer. Christmas Day was a day of solitude for me, spent reminiscing about Christmases past. The weather was unusually mild and spring-like for late December. I put on my windbreaker and took a long walk. On Boxing Day, I ate a buffet lunch with my good friend Gall, a breast cancer survivor. Since we had both survived life-threatening situations, we drew strength from each other, and she gave me lots of encouragement. I managed to get through Christmas and New Year's, but I found the Holidays only seemed to magnify my feelings of loneliness more intensely. I found it comforting to reconnect and socialize with my friends again and was trying hard to make a conscious effort not to isolate myself too much. At first, it was hard to adjust to going to shopping malls and restaurants the three of us used to go to together. Being alone in restaurants during festive times intensified my sense of longing. Seeing others enjoying moments with their spouses or families heightened the contrast with my solitary presence. Going to a restaurant solo proved to be less enjoyable; the experience brought bittersweet memories to the forefront. Imagining the joyous times when I shared meals with Sedrick and my dad created a poignant mix of nostalgia and sorrow.

Walking through the hallway in the Rideau Centre, where I first met Sedrick many years ago, made me miss him even more. Many things reminded me of him everywhere I went. Even though my family was now small, I made it a point to keep in touch with my cousins, Megan and Mary-Jane, who both live in Michigan, just outside Detroit. Dad used to correspond with them by letter for many years. My Uncle Bill, who was their father, shared a deep bond with my dad. Unfortunately, he passed away from cancer before I was born, so I never had the opportunity to meet him. The weight of grief had a profound impact on both my body and mind, emphasizing the significance of incorporating regular exercise into my routine to help cope with the emotional challenges.

I continued to work out with light weights at least every other day. It gave me a sense of freedom to go for long walks again every day without fearing for my own life. I was lucky that my apartment building was close to the Ottawa Parkway, which runs alongside the Ottawa River. Whenever I went out for a walk, I took extra time to notice the beauty of all the birds, the trees, and the water. Spending time in nature was very soothing and helped calm my nerves. There was also an outdoor swimming pool where I was living, so I could use it when summer came. I had always been a creative person and used to enjoy hobbies such as knitting and cross-stitch. After the trauma, I observed a shift in myself, struggling with prolonged concentration on any task. This made it challenging to dive back into my cherished hobbies, especially those requiring intricate details and focus. Despite the time it takes, I held onto hope that one day, my passion for these activities would rekindle. Thankfully, my cat Mojo became a source of comfort, and I was grateful I brought him with me from Jamaica.

    Having a pet to nurture lifted my spirits and eased some of the loneliness, and he was like my emotional support animal. I enjoyed having him curl up on my lap when I watched television. The nice thing about pets is they give you pure, unconditional love. Living back in a rental apartment again after being in a spacious house was an adjustment, but it was a good starting point for me. The building I lived in was very convenient and located right next to a major shopping mall. In my new place, I appreciated the convenience of having banks, restaurants, and accessible bus routes nearby for easy navigation around the city. However, my thoughts often drifted back to the house in Jamaica, filling me with a sense of sorrow. What I missed the most was the breathtaking million-dollar view of the sea and the joy of tending to a vibrant, tropical flower garden. The contrast stirred a mix of emotions as I adjusted to this new chapter in my life.

    The weather in Jamaica is always warm year-round, with gentle trade winds blowing off the sea. You can live in your summer clothes all year round. I thought I would spend the rest of my life in Jamaica with Sedrick, running our little tour bus together and enjoying the life that we had both worked so hard for.

Reflecting on what could have been, I couldn't escape the realization that if circumstances had unfolded as they were meant to, we would still be enjoying our time there together. However, fate took an unexpected turn, and I found myself back in the chilly climate of Canada once more. The irony of life's twists and turns hit me hard, bringing a mix of nostalgia and acceptance of the stark changes in my journey.

Life, as it often does, came full circle in ways I hadn't anticipated.

Donna M. McCully

Chapter 22
The Relentless Grip of Grief and Trauma

Loss is a chapter in the book of life, and with every turn of the page, we discover the resilience of the human spirit.

Grieving is a personal journey, and everyone experiences it uniquely. No one else can dictate how long or in what way a person should mourn because there's no set timeframe for grief. It's an individual process, and you have the right to go through it on your own terms, free from judgment. In my case, I had both good and bad days. The memories of Dad and Sedrick would sometimes overwhelm me, leading to uncontrollable tears. Despite the passage of over two years since losing Sedrick and more than a year since Dad's passing, the intensity of raw emotions remained unchanged.

I learned it was better to cry than to hold back the tears. Tears are a healthy part of the healing process. You should never feel bad about it. I read in a brochure that grief is not a sign of weakness but is just a sign of how much we cared for and loved the person we lost. The trauma that I experienced affected me greatly. Even after returning to Ottawa, I found myself haunted by nightmares. One particularly distressing dream involved Sedrick being held in a prison camp, facing execution by a firing squad. In this unsettling scenario, I was there for his last meal, watching him in the distance, clad in a bathrobe. The dream was a whirlwind of emotions, marked by my tears and desperate attempts to find a way to help him escape. The vividness and emotional impact lingered even after waking up, leaving me grappling with the residual distress from the dream.

    The dream left me feeling very upset and shaken, which made it almost impossible to get back to sleep. I was also very security-conscious. Once someone had broken into your home and tried to kill you, I think that fear always stays with you. I always double-checked if I had locked my door whenever I came home and would check again before bed. There was an underground parking garage in the apartment building, and every time I walked through it, I looked around to see if anybody was following me. There are criminals everywhere, and I was keenly aware of my surroundings. Ottawa is not without its share of crimes either, nor, for that matter, is any city. Loud bangs still startled me, and seeing young men wearing hoodies affected me. If a young man with a hoodie walked toward me on the sidewalk, I would cross the street to avoid them. I could not bear the sight of blood. These were just reminders that triggered those familiar feelings of angst for me. I had a lot of flashbacks where the events of that day played out with vivid intensity, as if it had just happened. The memory of witnessing the brutal and violent death of a loved one is not something that fades easily. Even with the passage of time, the recollection of those horrifying moments can resurface, triggering a nauseating sensation deep in the stomach. When these waves of grief hit, there's a recognition that the pain remains, and in those moments, I allow myself to experience the intense emotions that come with the memories.

    I usually sat quietly and reminded myself that I was somewhere safe and no one could hurt me. Then, I started doing some deep breathing exercises until calmness returned. The magnitude of this type of grief was, at times, very overwhelming, but I was trying my best to deal with it. When you're mourning the loss of your loved ones or if you're struggling with your mental health, it's crucial to have someone to share your feelings with. After the deaths of Sedrick and my dad, I never had any type of grief counselling or therapy until after I returned to Ottawa. Handling the aftermath of such traumatic experiences proved challenging, and I attempted to navigate through it on my own initially. Utilizing self-help resources like books on grief and Post Traumatic Stress Disorder (PTSD) from the library was my initial approach. However, recognizing the need for professional support, I consulted a family doctor at the Appletree Clinic who then referred me to a psychiatrist. The official diagnosis of both PTSD and depression shed light on the mental health challenges I was facing. Although a prescription for antidepressants was provided, I hesitated to fill it at that time.

I was worried about the potential side effects of these medications and decided that I wanted to see a therapist instead. After searching online, I found the website for Family Services Ottawa. They have a free walk-in counselling office and offer a single session with an experienced counsellor. I booked an appointment to go and see them, and they provided me with the name and telephone number of Dr. Jenny Love, a therapist and social worker who has done a lot of work with victims of crime. The counsellor suggested that she would be able to assist me in dealing with the PTSD and depression that I had suffered as a result of everything that I had endured. Recognizing the necessity for professional help, I reached out to Dr. Love and began attending psychotherapy sessions. Dr. Love elucidated that my grief was complicated due to the violent nature of Sedrick's death. This meant not only mourning his loss but also grappling with the circumstances surrounding his demise. Engaging in trauma-informed care, Dr. Love equipped me with valuable tools and strategies to manage triggers and navigate through the complexities of grief. These sessions became a crucial support in coping with the emotional aftermath.

The therapy that I received helped improve my outlook on life and reduced some of the symptoms of my PTSD. There is a moving ceremony that Bereaved Families of Ottawa holds at Beechwood Cemetery every year at the end of May. You can purchase butterflies for your deceased loved ones, and their names are read out loud at the service. A musician plays soothing harp music during the ceremony, and then the butterflies are released. Afterward, there is a walk around the cemetery that allows you the opportunity to reflect. I attended the ceremony with my friend Mona and purchased two butterflies, one for Sedrick and one for Dad. This service was powerful and meaningful in its symbolism, and I found it to be a deep, spiritual experience. The release of the butterflies represents the idea that even in death, there is the potential for rebirth and transformation. It also symbolizes the release of your departed loved one's spirit. During this time, I tried to surround myself with people who would encourage me and give me moral support. I needed caring, compassionate people who would validate my feelings. They didn't have to say anything to me; they just had to be there to listen or hug me. Dealing with the emotional impact of the double loss had been very tough for me, but I was fighting to climb out of the pit of darkness.

Chapter 23
The Murder Investigation

When the storm subsides, you cherish the calm...until you realize it isn't over.

The lingering question of "why" has been a constant companion since the tragedy. The haunting final words spoken by Sedrick have become an unsettling presence in my thoughts, leaving me to wonder if he recognized one of the attackers. The fact that they were masked and silent adds to the mystery, creating an uncomfortable suspicion that I might know the gunman. There's an eerie familiarity, particularly in the eyes, that nags at me, prompting Lily to share a similar sentiment, feeling that she, too, might recognize the assailant. The uncertainty and potential familiarity only deepen the emotional turmoil surrounding the incident.

That has to be more than just a coincidence. To this date, the bullet fragment recovered in the stuffing of the sofa has not matched up to any firearm. Every time the police recover a stolen gun in Jamaica, the crime lab runs ballistics tests to see whether or not there is a match. The case would be wide open if they could just find the murder weapon. Sometimes, I wonder if the killers tossed the gun into the sea. The police have never recovered the knife used in the attack either. When the police were in our home on the day of the homicide, I gave them the serial number as well as all the information on our Toshiba laptop computer so that their Cyber Crimes Unit could run a trace on it. They have never found the computer. The loss of the computer, seemingly taken as a trophy or potentially sold for parts, adds another layer of distress to an already tragic situation. The lingering suspicion that the death threats received months earlier may be connected to Sedrick's murder intensifies the emotional burden. While refraining from delving into specific details due to the ongoing case, the hurtful words and threats from a neighbor remain vivid in memory, contributing to the overall anguish and sense of vulnerability. The unresolved nature of these events amplifies the emotional weight, leaving questions and a pervasive unease.

    We were so scared that we drove to the police station to report the incident. Unfortunately, death threats are not taken seriously by the police in Jamaica. The police sergeant at the station merely called him on the telephone and reprimanded him, but that was all he ever did. Whoever had attempted to break into our home the first time could well be the same ones who came back and committed the murder. One of my neighbors told me that several laborers hired to build our house were from the town just up the road. The realization that the perpetrators had intimate knowledge of your home's layout intensifies the distress, raising concerns about the potential involvement of someone familiar with your living space. The detective's inquiry about any animosity within the JUTA Tour company, driven by Sedrick's success as a new driver, introduces a possibility of professional jealousy. However, the reassurance from Sedrick's close friend within JUTA Tours, attesting to Sedrick's likability among the drivers, provides a contrasting perspective. This ambiguity adds a layer of complexity to the emotional toll, as you grapple with uncertainties surrounding the motive and the identities of those involved.

Life Interrupted

Whenever other bus drivers were waiting to pick up passengers for a return trip from Montego Bay Airport, they talked and joked with him. I heard that his nickname amongst the drivers was The American because they used to tease him about his accent. I had given the detectives a list of just a handful of people that we knew who I felt may have possibly had some involvement in the murder. The detective's promise to locate and question the individuals responsible likely stirred a mix of hope and anxiety. The expectation that he would interview the neighbor who had previously threatened you intensified the emotional stakes, as this person could potentially hold valuable information. The omission of this step from the detective's actions might have left you feeling confused and frustrated, grappling with the desire for justice and answers. I was told that another neighbor did happen to overhear some information that could have helped with the case. The revelation about someone in the area possessing pertinent information could have reignited a glimmer of hope, mingled with the ongoing uncertainty and emotional turmoil surrounding the unresolved case.

Unfortunately, in Jamaica, people tend to withhold information because they are too afraid to come forward for fear of retaliation. I considered putting up a reward on the Jamaica Crime Stop program in the hope that a person or persons would finally come forward with information that could lead to an arrest if they knew they would get compensated for it. There is even a reluctance to call Crime Stop. It is linked primarily to the idea that if you are an informer, you are dead, a belief that prevails on the island. Even though the tips are anonymous, they cannot guarantee the safety of the tipster in case their identity gets shared with the police. When people in the communities do not stand up and speak out about what they know, these criminals virtually get away with murder. It only puts the lives of other innocent people at risk as well, and the cycle of violence continues. I also worried that putting up a reward could endanger the lives of relatives who still lived in Jamaica, so I did not go ahead.

Crime Stop has confirmed that the number of arrests recorded during its 34-year existence is less than 10 percent of the calls it has received since then, which is a very discouraging statistic. Another option I explored was to hire a private investigator in Jamaica, but a disadvantage would be the expense without guarantee of an arrest ever being made. Their credentials would need to be verified to find one that has a rock-solid reputation for solving murder cases. I would not want to pay a lot of money to a private detective only to discover they are not getting any further than the police on the investigation. I have to be able to support myself financially, so I had to put that idea on the back burner.

While I was still living on the island, there were a few meetings between myself and the investigating officer about the murder. After one year, there were no arrests, and a few more months passed without a break in the case. I got in touch with Superintendent Reynolds, who would oversee the case. I went to the Port Maria Police Station in person at least once a month to meet with him and Detective Steele to ask for regular updates. I wanted to ensure they would not put the case file away in a drawer and forget about it. They both assured me that they would do their best to try and get it solved even though sometimes they do not always catch the perpetrators. After returning to Canada, I started to search for some resources that could assist me with my quest for justice, and I found the website for the Canadian Resource Centre for Victims of Crime. I contacted them, and they provided advocacy services on my behalf.

They sent letters addressed to the Canadian Minister of Foreign Affairs, the Prime Minister's Office, and the Police Commissioner of the Jamaican Police Constabulary Force. As well, I also attended a few Loss to Violence Support Group meetings that were held monthly by the CRCVC. It was somewhat comforting to be in a room with other people who were in the same boat as me in terms of having lost a loved one to a violent crime. We had all joined an exclusive club that none of us ever wanted to join.

I became friends with a wonderful woman named Jill, whose son Brian was a murder victim, and we started meeting for coffee or lunch regularly. I also inquired whether or not it would be possible to get some assistance from Interpol. I had hoped that our Canadian government could provide the local Jamaican police with advice or could assist with the investigation in some way.

Unfortunately, our government does not interfere in local police matters, and this proved to be a dead end. All victims of crime may exercise their rights under The Canadian Victims Bill of Rights (CVBR) while in Canada. If a Canadian becomes victimized while abroad, they are entirely at the mercy of the local police and justice system of that country. Whenever we heard about a murder in the news, Sedrick used to have a favourite expression. He said that time is longer than rope, and whatever goes around comes around. These guys might run, but their time will come. They cannot hide forever. A retired policeman in Jamaica told me a story one day about a man confessing to a murder that he had just committed. The detective was working on a homicide case and started questioning the suspect at the police station. Suddenly, the man began to cry like a baby and opened up to him about killing the person.

The man's decision to approach the detective and express a desire to unburden his soul about the murder is a complex mix of guilt, moral conflict, and a potential sense of responsibility. This revelation introduces a layer of hope, as it opens a possibility for the conscience of Sedrick's killers to weigh on them, potentially leading to a confession. The emotional weight carried by the murderers, coupled with the potential impact on the case, adds a nuanced layer to the ongoing pursuit of justice. For you, this development may bring a blend of anticipation, anxiety, and the lingering hope for closure as you navigate the uncertain path of the investigation.

Chapter 24
Lessons Learned About Moving Abroad

In the garden of remembrance, every tear shed becomes a nurturing rain, allowing the flowers of love to bloom eternally.

    I never want anyone to endure the agonizing ordeal I faced, and I feel compelled to share the harsh lessons I learned about moving abroad. The decision to relocate demands meticulous research and planning. The allure of a place during a vacation can be deceiving, as the reality of living in a foreign country unfolds in unexpected ways. Tourists have always been relatively safe in Jamaica, and the resorts have 24-hour security. We got caught up in the lure of the beautiful tropical island and the warm weather, but Sedrick hadn't lived in his country for 32 years.

    There are still many good people in Jamaica, but violent crime has increased there a lot. You have to be extra careful about your safety, no matter which country you choose to go and live in. We would have been better off living in a gated community with other expatriates and 24-hour security. It would have been a good idea to check the crime rate in the surrounding neighborhoods before moving there. Although we chose an upscale neighborhood, there were no security gates at either end of the roads leading into our area. It meant that people were constantly walking through the neighborhood on our street on their way to the next town. There were quite a few undeveloped lots in our area, which were very bushy, and paying someone to come and chop down the bushes in the empty lot next door could have prevented anyone from hiding there. We never asked for referrals or references from local businesses in the area when we planned to hire people to work on our house and yard. Instead, we just hired people by word of mouth. Local people would occasionally wander through our neighborhood, seeking work.

Despite not knowing any of them, we took a chance. The police later informed me that in most murder cases, it is often someone familiar with the victims. A significant oversight was our failure to install a security system, even though several security companies had provided brochures. It should have been a priority right after moving in – perhaps it could have deterred a potential intruder. While we had a few bright lights outside the house, it proved insufficient. Sedrick had discussed installing a camera system with a security company owner about a week before his tragic death, but, unfortunately, it might have been too late.

We always locked our doors, but it was not good enough, and the metal burglar bars surrounding the front porch should have had a padlock on them at all times. I never knew someone could kick in the doors to get into our house. Even though I didn't like guns, it would have been well worth it if it meant that Sedrick was better able to protect himself and his family. An alternative would have been to buy some good guard dogs for the yard. If we had a couple of Rottweilers or Dobermans, it may have helped us. People say that in Jamaica, criminals are even more afraid of being bitten by a dog than they are of getting shot. The two men probably would not have taken the chance to jump over the wall into our yard if they knew we had some aggressive dogs. Unfortunately, our dog Sandy was still a puppy then, and they must have known they would not be in danger of getting bitten. I wish we had known about the criminal justice system in Jamaica, and I found out that the Jamaican police operate much differently than in Canada.

They often do not have enough resources available to assist you. Before we ever decided to move there, we should have thought long and hard about what would happen if we found ourselves in a life-threatening situation and we needed to call the police. Something else we should have done when we first moved overseas was inform the Canadian High Commission and give them our new address. Maybe they could have assisted us after someone threatened our lives. It is a horrible experience to become a victim of a violent crime while living in a foreign country. Having a house by the seaside was beautiful, but it was a lot of work. The sea salt in Jamaica causes anything made of metal to rust very quickly. We constantly had to repaint the gates and the burglar bars after we moved in.

Applying marine paint was not just a financial strain, but it also consumed a significant amount of our time. Opting for one of the condominiums would have spared us from this struggle, requiring only a monthly maintenance fee, and providing more time for leisure. Above all, it would have ensured our safety. Reflecting on it, if we had moved after the initial break-in attempt, my husband would still be alive today. This realization is something I grapple with, and it's a burden I'll carry for the rest of my life.

Chapter 25
Putting Down New Roots

Though tears may blur our vision, the heart remembers every shared laugh, every tender touch, a mosaic of love that remains unbroken.

The process of selling my house in Jamaica proved to be a source of constant frustration. While I did receive several offers, most of them lacked the seriousness required for a successful deal. Each time a potential buyer withdrew their offer, it felt like a crushing disappointment, and my hopes were repeatedly dashed. I vividly remember a long-distance call from my real estate agent, who shared news of a potential client—a Jamaican author. This person expressed interest in staying in the house for a couple of weeks without any charges. While it sounded promising, the uncertainty of it all added another layer of emotional turmoil to an already challenging situation.

She said she wanted to make a cash offer if I agreed with the proposal. I did not have a good feeling about it, and I told my realtor that I could not agree because it sounded rather suspicious to me. While living in Jamaica, I heard horror stories about people pretending to be potential home buyers asking to stay in a seller's home for a few days and then refusing to leave! The prospect of dealing with squatters added another layer of stress to an already overwhelming situation. The mere thought of having to involve the police or go through legal processes to remove them was daunting, considering everything I had already endured. The house, once a place of joy, had become a financial burden in addition to the emotional toll. Alongside covering rent in Ottawa, I found myself shouldering the responsibility of property taxes on the Jamaican house. To ensure its upkeep, I sent money every month to a couple in Jamaica tasked with cleaning the house and maintaining the yard. The weight of these financial obligations only added to the emotional strain I was experiencing.

Finally, after what felt like an eternity, I received a valid offer and readily accepted it. Selling the house made me feel like I was able to cut ties with it and that I could move forward with my life to some degree. Once the sale was final, I began to look for a condo to purchase in Ottawa. In May 2019, I bought a cute, comfortable 2-bedroom unit that was perfect for me. The building is near shopping, major bus routes, and a bicycle path. Being able to purchase a home alone felt like a great accomplishment, and I settled in very nicely. In the Fall of 2019, I volunteered for the annual Salvation Army Christmas Kettle Campaign and the Ottawa Food Bank. It felt great going into the community and supporting these amazing charitable organizations.

I wanted to continue volunteer work, but these activities stopped temporarily when the COVID-19 pandemic started. Interestingly, I rekindled my love of knitting during the COVID-19 lockdown. Amid the challenging times of the pandemic, I found solace and purpose in knitting. Crafting a few afghans for dear friends and baby blankets for premature infants in the NICU became not just a creative outlet but a source of comfort during these tumultuous times. After the devastating losses I experienced, hobbies had lost their appeal, making the return of my love for knitting all the more meaningful. The rhythmic motion of the needles became a therapeutic escape, helping to alleviate stress and anxiety, and I continue to cherish this renewed passion.

Chapter 26
Surviving Breast Cancer

As we navigate the vast sea of grief, may the waves of memories carry us towards shores of healing and acceptance.

In May 2022, my world was once again thrust into chaos. A routine mammogram revealed a daunting presence on my left breast, demanding additional tests. The subsequent rounds of examinations, including a second mammogram, a breast ultrasound, and a needle biopsy, unraveled a harsh reality — I was diagnosed with a rare form of breast cancer known as adenoid cystic carcinoma. The weight of this revelation shook me to the core, unleashing a flood of emotions and uncertainties.

Luckily, it was Stage 1 cancer, which meant that it had not spread to any of my lymph nodes. ACC forms mostly in glandular tissue in the head and neck. It often starts in the salivary glands in the neck, mouth, or throat and can also form in other parts of the body, such as the breast or prostate gland. This type of cancer is not considered hereditary. I never smoked a day in my life, I've always been physically active, and I've been following a pescatarian diet for over 25 years. I was shocked and blindsided by the diagnosis. The mysterious origins of adenoid cystic carcinoma elude our understanding, with ongoing research hinting at genetic transformations throughout one's life as a potential culprit. As I grappled with my cancer diagnosis, the weight of the journey ahead, I kept a silent reserve about the haunting specter of Sedrick's murder when discussing it with the radiologist. The intertwining complexities of life's challenges added an emotional layer to my already tumultuous experience.

I couldn't help but wonder if there was a connection between my having PTSD and the development of cancer. Maybe it was a weird coincidence, and I just happened to be one of the unlucky women who developed breast cancer. I don't know for sure, but I do know that Sedrick's murder affected my health mentally and physically. When I was officially diagnosed with PTSD, I remember the doctor telling me that PTSD keeps the body in a constant state of hyperarousal, which can cause changes to the immune system. I wanted to get as much information as I could to try and better understand my cancer. There isn't much information about adenoid cystic carcinoma since it is such a rare form of cancer. In my quest for understanding, I stumbled upon a revelation that struck a chord. American medical studies unfolded a potential link between the echoes of PTSD and the emergence of cancer. The stark findings revealed that survivors of trauma bear a heightened vulnerability to a spectrum of health challenges – from cardiovascular struggles to respiratory, gastroenteric battles, and, poignantly, the haunting Specter of breast cancer. This revelation added an emotional layer to my already complex journey, leaving me grappling with the intricate dance of mental and physical well-being.

There was another study that found that women who experienced symptoms of PTSD at some point in their lives had a twofold risk of developing ovarian cancer compared with women who never had any PTSD symptoms. The surgical oncologist discussed my treatment options with me, and I had the choice between a lumpectomy or a mastectomy. I chose to have a lumpectomy followed by a course of radiation treatments. My surgery was on August 2, 2022, and the radiation treatments began in early October, five days a week for six weeks. The surgical intervention and subsequent treatments emerged triumphant in vanquishing the insidious presence of every cancer cell within me. Yet, this victory does not signal the end but inaugurates an everlasting vigil. An annual pilgrimage to the realm of mammograms and breast ultrasounds now marks my journey, an unyielding scrutiny to ensure the specter of cancer does not dare to resurface. In this dance with uncertainty, the radiologist delicately introduced the prospect of Hormone Replacement Therapy, a nuanced strategy to safeguard against the lurking shadows of cancer's return. The emotional gravity of this ongoing vigilance echoes in the chambers of my life, a symphony of hope. I was born with a hole in my heart, had a blood clot in my leg in 2007, and suffered a TIA (ministroke) in 2017.

      Therefore, I will always have an increased risk of blood clots and stroke. Hormone therapy could further increase this risk for me, so we both agreed that I was not a good candidate for HRT. Having gone through breast cancer was a very frightening experience, but I kept a very positive attitude throughout my cancer journey. After being diagnosed, I reminded myself that I am a fighter and I could get through this battle as well. Early detection of the cancer was the key. I made it through the tough battle with breast cancer. Regular check-ups like mammograms and self-exams played a crucial role in catching it early. Grateful to be a survivor, and it emphasizes how these simple screenings can make a big difference in saving lives.

Donna M. McCully

Chapter 27
10 Years After Sedrick's Murder

The echo of laughter, the shadow of a smile, are like whispers of love, assuring us that the ones we miss are never truly gone.

On November 17, 2023, it was a whole decade since Sedrick's tragic murder. Strangely, the pain felt as fresh as if it had just occurred. In search of a meaningful tribute, I was invited to speak to Victimology students at Algonquin College. Emotions ran high as I shared our story, reflecting on the lasting impact of that fateful day.

Talking about his murder has gotten easier for me over time. A few years ago, I would not have been able to speak publicly about it without breaking down. The experience was very therapeutic for me, and I was able to shed some light on what you go through as a homicide survivor. As well, I have the unique perspective of being the survivor of an attempted homicide. I have firsthand knowledge of what it feels like when someone is trying to murder you and the terror that you go through when you think you are just about to die. I am very fortunate that I lived to tell my story. The teacher expressed gratitude for my visit and later emailed me with positive feedback from the students. Hearing that, I felt a sense of fulfillment. If sharing my story can help others, I'm open to more speaking engagements. None of us expects such tragedies to happen to us, but the sad reality is that every day, someone, somewhere becomes a victim of violence.

I have seen and experienced the dark, evil side of humanity firsthand, and it is a horrible feeling to know that the people responsible for your loved ones' demise are still freely walking the streets. After all the love and kindness that Sedrick showed me during our marriage and for putting up a fight to try and save his family that day, the least I can do for him is to try and find the killers. These men have taken so much away from me, and they have caused so much suffering and heartache to those left behind to pick up the pieces. Catching them will not bring him back, but it would give some sense of closure for his family and me. They have been asking me if there has been any progress on the case, but sadly, there are still no answers for them. There have been no new leads at all or any new evidence.

The case is now cold, and I have found that dealing with the Jamaican police and legal system can be exhausting and, at times, very frustrating. Seeking justice takes time, and the journey can be long, but I won't give up. Sedrick can't speak for himself now, so I've become his voice. Around once a month, I send emails to the Case Worker for Jamaica at Global Affairs Canada, asking for updates from the Jamaican Police. Trying to reach the Jamaican Police directly has been unfruitful, so I find this indirect method more accessible. Hoping that one day, the justice system will give us closure. Yet, the thought of going through a trial is daunting. It would mean reliving the horrors of that day. If I ever testify in Jamaica, I'd require a police escort for safety to and from the courthouse.

Before I left Jamaica, the police had informed me that the families of killers sometimes murder witnesses to prevent them from going to court to testify. I would be more than willing to go on the stand and give my testimony, and I will have to be brave and cross that bridge if and when the time ever comes. There may be a way that I could even testify remotely. I would like to see them being held accountable for this heinous crime. It's not just about catching the two men who committed the murder; those who planned and set us up need to face consequences too. If I had the chance, I'd ask them why they took my husband's life and tried to take mine. Holding them accountable is crucial to prevent such tragedy for others. I dream of standing at Sedrick's graveside, telling him that his killers will spend their lives in prison, bringing some closure to this painful chapter.

I've learned to live with Sedrick's murder and my attempted murder by mentally putting the events of that day on a shelf until needed. I do tend to replay the whole deadly home invasion all over again in my mind on the anniversary date. The way he died was also a part of his life. I just let the awful memories wash over me. Then, I look through our photo albums and remember our beautiful life together. Sedrick was a very cheerful man, and he was always smiling in all of his pictures. This is how I want to remember him—loving, a great son, brother, uncle, cousin, the one I loved deeply, and the heart of my world. He's unique, and I'll forever hold him close. I feel fortunate to have shared twenty-eight years of marriage with this amazing man. Not everyone gets to experience true love like we did, and even though life can be tough, I still wanted to spend every moment with him.

Although no longer inundated with flashbacks and recurring nightmares, I'm still very vigilant and aware of my surroundings, and I think I always will be. When someone comes knocking on my door, I first look through the peephole to see who it is. I won't answer the door unless I recognize the person or expect a home delivery. Unless I go somewhere with friends who pick me up and bring me back home, I no longer like to go out at night. Loud bangs, like fireworks, still give me a start, bringing back memories of gunshots. It's a lingering effect from the trauma, but things are improving, largely due to the fantastic therapy I've received. It took a long time, but I've managed to stop blaming myself for what happened.

    I had feelings of guilt and a distorted sense of responsibility for a very long time. Finally, I realized there was nothing else I could have done differently that day to change the outcome. I did the only thing I could have done, which was grab my cell phone, run upstairs, and call the police. I was able to shift the blame squarely onto the shoulders of the killers where it rightfully belongs. I've learned not to get too stressed over circumstances beyond my control. The deaths of Sedrick and my dad left a gaping hole in my heart, and there is nothing that could ever fill the void left by their passing. My very soul was deeply wounded and permanently scarred. Christmas and birthdays are when I miss them the most. That is when their absence is most glaring, and my memories and the love I had for them will always remain strong. You never get over losing someone you love, but the pain gradually lessens over time. Looking at the moon reminds me of Sedrick and Dad. They both loved it so much. I believe their souls have gone to Heaven and are both at peace. I hope Sedrick and my dad have reunited with our ancestors. They're forever in my heart, and at times, I sense their presence. To honor their memory, I've participated in the Rideau Valley Conservation Foundation's Memorial Tree Program. They plant seedlings on your behalf in forested areas as a tribute to your loved ones.

Life Interrupted

The seedlings are cared for over several years until they can take their place in a new forest. I donated to have two seedlings planted in memory of Sedrick and Dad. Getting the trees planted is a physical reminder that their legacy continues even though their physical bodies are gone. Knowing that the trees will go on providing clean air, a safe habitat for wildlife, and peace is comforting to me. It is important to tell your loved ones how much you love them, spend as much quality time as possible with them, and hug them often. We can never predict what's coming or how much time we have. Life is short and can slip away in an instant. Let's not spend our time on grudges, trivial matters, anger, or negativity. Instead, aim to spread love, kindness, and compassion whenever you can. We're all linked to the universe and each other.

When I look at my reflection in the mirror, I see a woman who used to be a loving wife and daughter. All I have left of that former life are my photographs and precious memories. It has been difficult for me to have to address myself as a widow because it is a term that I don't like. I've regained a sense of normalcy, although everything about my life has completely changed. I am no longer the same person that I used to be. Now, I live moment by moment, one day at a time, and try not to make too many long-range plans anymore. I appreciate each new day as it comes, finding joy and happiness in simple things like a walk-in nature, listening to music, seeing friends, or enjoying a nice meal in a restaurant. The first thing I do when I wake up in the morning is thank God for another day. He does have a will and a purpose for my life, and He spared my life for a reason. I want to channel my energy into trying to do some good to help others with whatever time I have left on this planet. Life took an unexpected turn, but here I am, still standing. I've survived. The human spirit is tougher than we realize. You discover your strength when being strong is your only option. Faith has taught me that even in the darkest moments, we find courage and grow. The song "Rise Up" by Andra Day keeps me going, its words pushing me forward. I could have given up, but instead, I chose to rise and face life. I feel like I can overcome anything. I'm slowly piecing my life back together with grace, dignity, and gratitude. Sedrick and my dad would want me to be happy, and I want to make them proud. Losing a loved one is incredibly painful, but you can make it through.

I have been there and understand the full impact of the immense suffering that is caused by losing the ones we love, and the murder of a loved one adds a whole other dimension of grief. I have learned that you must be gentle with yourself and treat yourself kindly. It is okay not to be okay, and please know that you do not have to struggle alone with your thoughts and feelings. You should reach out to the people who care about you or go and see a doctor and let them know how you are feeling. Reaching out for help is a sign of strength, not weakness. No matter how dark things seem, there is always hope for the future. There are many good resources available for counselling, and you should not be afraid to seek help if you are having difficulty coping or experiencing symptoms of depression, anxiety, or thoughts about suicide. If you're feeling suicidal, please reach out right away – it could save your life. You're important, and help is available. The International Association for Suicide Prevention has resources to connect you with assistance in your country. You can reach out to a crisis hotline, which operates 24/7, or visit the emergency room at your nearest hospital. Writing about my traumatic experiences was a deeply emotional journey, and I shed many tears along the way. One day, shortly after the murder, an unexplained force compelled me to write, and I just felt the need to share my story. When I sat in front of the computer, the words seemed to flow effortlessly. Before long, I found that I had written a few chapters, and I continued to add more as time went on. Putting my thoughts, feelings, and emotions about the events in writing has been a powerful outlet for me, and I would encourage anyone coping with grief to write their feelings down, even if it's in a journal.

To everyone who has lost a loved one, may you find comfort, strength, and hope as you travel on your grief journey. I stand with you, and I empathize with you completely.

www.ingramcontent.com/pod-product-compliance
Lightning Source LLC
Chambersburg PA
CBHW041305240426
43661CB00011B/1021